Jackie Jarvis is a business own[er]
who regularly applies the Qui[ck]
to both her own business an[d]
ambitious business-owner cli[ents].

Before becoming a business mentor, Jackie gained
experience across a range of different industries in both
the SME and corporate environments. She has worked for
both top corporate brands and small start-up companies

Jackie has a wealth of first-hand experience as a sales-
person, a sales manager, a marketing manager, a training
manager, an executive coach and now as a business owner
herself. She is a director of Heart of Business, a unique
concept, created with her two business partners, that
brings together a team of like-minded business mentors
and professional service providers, who all share the
desire to make a difference through the work they do.

Jackie also works within her own independent brand
'Jackie Jarvis', coaching business owners and professionals to win the business they aspire to in an 'authentic'
manner.

www.heart-of-business.co.uk
www.jackiejarvis.co.uk

Also by Constable & Robinson

The Small Business Start-up Workbook

Start and Run a Business from Home

How to Make Sales when you Don't Like Selling

How to Manage Difficult People

Prepare to Sell Your Company

Owner's Guide to a Small Business Website

Quick Wins in Sales and Marketing for Ambitious Business Owners

Jackie Jarvis

ROBINSON

First published in Great Britain in 2015 by Robinson

A CIP catalogue record for this book
is available from the British Library.

ISBN 978-1-84528-613-2 (paperback)
ISBN: 978-1-47211-922-3 (ebook)

Typeset in Great Britain by SX Composing DTP, Rayleigh, Essex
Printed and bound by CPI Group (UK) Ltd, Croydon, CR0 4YY

Robinson
is an imprint of
Constable & Robinson Ltd
100 Victoria Embankment
London EC4Y 0DY

An Hachette UK Company
www.hachette.co.uk

www.constablerobinson.com

This book is dedicated to all my wonderful business owner clients and contacts who, over the years, have taught me as much I have helped them, if not more.

You are the ones who have made all the ideas in this book come alive and mean something in the real world of business. I am honoured to have been your guide on your journey.

Thank you so much. It has been a pleasure and a joy to have worked with you, and – for those reading this book with whom I am currently working – continues to be so.

Acknowledgements

With grateful thanks to my partner, Matt Wright, who has worked tirelessly editing each *Quick Win*, as well as giving me those all-important positive words of encouragement which I appreciate very much.

His ideas and insights also helped to craft the structure and style of the book.

Preface

I know what life is like for most busy business owners – it can be a real struggle to have the time or motivation to pick up a book.

This book has been written with those challenges in mind. It aims to inspire you, with an easy structure to follow, jargon-free language, stimulating quotes with questions, and winning formulas which will transform your business.

Quick ideas
Each of the 50 Quick Wins gives you a quick introduction to the idea, Quick Questions for reflection, a Quick Win formula to follow, a Quick Success story and some practical Quick Actions for you to take.

Quick read
The book has been designed with you in mind – to enable you to pick it up for inspiration or illumination, as and when required. I hope that it will sit on your desk and be referred to from time to time, not sit on a shelf gathering dust!

Quick results
This book contains real-life examples of the Quick Wins which I have helped ambitious business owners to implement and which get results. These are proven winning strategies which can work for you in your business.

Enjoy winning more business!

Jackie Jarvis

Contents

7 Quick Wins to Build Team Talent and Support

CHAPTER 1:
Quick Wins to Get on Track and Motivated

1. Analyse what isn't working and why
2. Decide what you want and clarify your 'why'
3. Create an inspiring vision
4. Set breakthrough goals
5. Value your time

1: Analyse what isn't working and why

'If something isn't working, don't be afraid to stop or change it.'

To thrive as a business, you must be able to attract and retain profitable customers – you will need sales and marketing in order to achieve that. If you are not currently attracting enough new leads, or winning enough new business, you need to ask yourself why this is, and then take the appropriate steps to put it right.

As a business development mentor, I have seen and heard many of the mistakes made by business owners, both large and small. These mistakes have resulted in a great deal of wasted time, expense and resources, as well as causing a lot of frustration along the way.

Typical mistakes

- Lack of a sales and marketing plan – haphazard activities

- Poor decisions about what to invest in – not enough research

- Starting with a website before thinking through your best target customer, what your service is, and how it works

- Trying to do too much, too quickly and making mistakes

- Outdated or weak brand identity which sends the wrong message

- Mixed marketing messages with no coherent theme

- An unclear or confusing proposition

- Relying on just one or two methods of generating business

- No sales follow-up system or proper record keeping

- Not keeping track of results

- Blindly carrying on, despite not achieving the desired results

- Trying to do it all yourself despite not having the skills

- Not investing in the expertise to get it right

- Not briefing or managing providers effectively

- Engaging providers and still doing it yourself.

Quick Questions

Which mistakes do you recognise from the list above?

What are these mistakes costing you?

Quick Win

Before you start making any changes, please be honest and ask yourself this: what is not working as well as it could?

Here are six questions to help evaluate your current sales and Marketing activities:

Where do your best sales leads come from?

What have you done in the past that used to generate leads, and how successful has this been?

What is not working well enough? Why is that? Do you know? And if you don't, how could you find out?

What is wasting the most time, money and effort?

What do you know that needs improving?

What help, resources or expertise do you require to get it right?

Quick Success

When I am mentoring business owners, our initial conversations often tend to centre upon what has worked in the past but is not working any more. A Quick Win here, for example, would be to stop spending money on sales and Marketing activities that are not generating results, until you have properly evaluated them. You can save thousands of pounds just by doing this. For example:

When I noticed that my newsletter and email marketing were no longer generating any significant return, I simply stopped them for six months. Nobody noticed. We saved time, money and effort – and then concentrated on putting a fresh plan in place.

When I analysed the personal sales time it took to sell places on a group small business programme I was running,

I realised that the time spent far outweighed the results we were achieving. So I changed the whole sales process and started selling places on the courses from one event. That worked a lot better for us.

Quick Actions

Make a list of all of your sales and marketing activities.

Estimate the time and cost for each activity versus the results you are getting.

Stop any costly activities that are not working.

Take time out to properly plan an effective Sales and Marketing strategy (the ideas in this book will help you do to this).

Get the expertise to help you deliver it.

Start measuring results so that you can fine-tune as you go along.

2: Decide what you want and clarify your 'why'

'Once you are sure you are on the right path, it is OK to run.'

When was the last time you stopped, took a deep breath and asked yourself the question. 'What do I want and why?'

Under pressure, it is often easier to start explaining what you don't want, but all that does is to reinforce the negative. In order to be able to move forward, it is essential to have a vision – a goal or an idea of how you would like things to be.

Knowing why you want what you want is vital, since this is the motivation that will keep you going when you feel tired and there are hills to climb.

Some people say they want to 'make a difference' with their business – they want to contribute in some way, or to do something important for the greater good. Their motivation goes well beyond just making money or a living from their business. Others say they are doing it for their families, or for personal ambition.

Either way, if you can connect with your 'why', your day-to-day activities will appear so much more important to you because you will know they are now linked to a bigger, more important picture. You will become more resilient and more determined to persevere, even when the going gets tough.

So, if you have lost your 'why', finding it again is important.

Quick Questions
Are you clear about what you want?

Do you know why you do what you do?

Quick Win
In order to be truly motivated to put the work in to grow a business, you need to know what you want and, most importantly, why you want it.

Questions to uncover your 'WHY?'

These questions will help you go a little deeper and uncover what is really motivating you and your business. Take some quiet time and use these questions to stimulate some thoughts.

What do you enjoy the most about your business and why?

What do you really want your business to be about?

What are you most passionate about in your business?

What do you want to contribute through your business?

What is important about the contribution you want to make?

Why is that important to you?

What is the difference you really want to make?

Why does that matter to you?

What is your strongest WHY?

These questions can be hard to answer sitting at a desk with a blank piece of paper in front of you, so go for a long walk and ponder them. Jot down any ideas that come to mind, or, if you are visual, draw some pictures.

Keep a notebook beside your bed and reflect upon these questions before you go to sleep. You may be surprised what you come up with – your 'why' is vital to you.

Quick Success

Kez was the director of a successful homemaking service for busy corporate mums. She achieved a real sense of purpose once she realised that her business drivers were closely connected to her personal experiences.

As a mother herself, Kez had been juggling her home life and bringing up two children, with her business life and climbing the career ladder. She loved her work and her kids, but it was a constant battle to combine them both.

Then Kez became ill and found herself at home, unable to do very much at all. She tried to find a company that offered the combination of homemaking help and a high-quality childcare service, but couldn't find any that delivered the kind of service she required. That experience triggered the idea to start her own business.

When Kez set up her homemaking service, she had a clear sense of who she was doing it for. Her purpose was to give busy corporate mums the freedom to pursue their career ambitions whilst maintaining a happy home.

Kez's 'why' was all about giving the women she related to the support they deserved. She felt it was what she had needed when she was pursuing her corporate career and now wanted to help other women in her position.

The important thing for Kez was that she connected fully with her customers, and the challenges they were facing, having had the same experiences herself. This became a driving force in her business, helping Kez to stay passionate and motivated whilst overcoming all the pains associated with growing a successful business.

Quick Actions

Share your WHY with your team members and your customers.

Make your WHY an important part of your business story.

Create something visual that will remind you of your WHY on a daily basis.

Make your WHY matter and be proud of it.

3: Create an inspiring vision

'Vision without execution is hallucination.'

Creating a vision is your way of anticipating the future. Think of it as planting a seed in your mind – if fed and watered properly, it will flower and grow over time in the way that it was always meant to.

Looking into the future in this way allows you to check whether you like what you see. Describing your vision can inspire both you and others in your team – everybody needs something to aim for. When you align your day-to-day activities with your vision, they will be more real and more meaningful.

To make this vision a reality, you will need to take action today. The daily choices you make will ultimately be the difference between you attaining your vision or staying put.

Simply having a vision is not enough to make it happen.

Quick Questions
Take a few moments to relax and take a walk into the future. Close your eyes and imagine yourself in this place where everything you wanted has been achieved.

What do you see happening in your business?

What does it look like?

What kind of clients do you see?

Who do you see working with you?

What are you doing?

What are people saying about your business?

Quick Win

It can be useful to get someone external to facilitate a 'vision session' with you and your team. When I work with clients we use something called a 'vision orbit' (a big three-ring circle), with colourful Post-it notes to help unravel thinking and gain clarity. I help clients to think about where they are now, in the key measurable areas of their business, and then project forwards to where they want to be in three years' time. This exercise always stimulates positive discussion.

Once you have a vision, you can use it to motivate both yourself and others – this is often the first step needed to kick-start a strategic planning meeting with your team. Your 'breakthrough business goals and objectives' (see Quick Win #4) should come out of this vision, and your strategic action plan should be guided by these goals.

Quick Success

Anne-Marie, the director of a successful PR and social media company, found the vision orbit session that we undertook at the beginning of her mentoring programme incredibly useful. She still has the vision orbit pinned up on the wall in her office, and it has guided every decision they have made as a business over this past year. The question is always: 'Is what we are choosing to do now taking us closer to our vision?' Being a highly creative company, having a clear vision of where they are headed as a business is vital both for Anne-Marie personally, and for her team.

Quick Actions

Take time out with your partners or team, and brainstorm the vision you have for your business.

Write a description.

Use a visual – a vision circle or a vision board. That way you can remind yourself of it from time to time, add to it, or adapt as things change. Find a visual image that you can relate to. Pin it up on the wall where you can see it every day – it will keep you anchored to your future.

Make sure the action you take is aligned with your vision.

4: Set breakthrough goals

'Goals are your promises to yourself – they will light your path and inspire your journey.'

A goal is a written statement of intent. It represents the target you are aiming for. There is far more commitment behind a written goal than behind one that merely remains as a thought in your head. The level of commitment you make to each goal influences the energy you will channel to make it happen.

'Breakthrough goals' are the goals that are the real keys to your success. They are the ones that will make the biggest difference and are most important to you – once you achieve them, everything else will seem possible.

Quick Questions
What are the three most important goals you intend to achieve this year?

Would any of them mean a 'breakthrough' for your business?

Quick Win
Your goals need to be SMART:

Specific

Measurable

Achievable

Relevant

Time-bound.

If they are SMART, you will be able to measure your achievement. However, if they are woolly – e.g. 'I want to grow my business and win more customers' – how will you know if you have ever achieved it? Does winning 'more customers' mean one more or fifty more?

Goals that remain vague ideas usually fail to be realised. Once you make the commitment to your goals and write them down, they are more likely to become a reality.

Take each breakthrough goal you want to achieve and break it down into the three 'How to' goals that will contribute to its achievement.

Keep it simple but make it measurable.

Breakthrough goals and the 'how to' goals required to make them happen

Breakthrough goal: Hit our £1 million turnover target

'How to' goals:
1) Win 10 new corporate client accounts worth £50K+ each
2) Increase existing client sales by 15 per cent through cross-selling
3) Sell advertising space on new website

Breakthrough goal: Build local brand awareness

'How to' goals:
1) Complete newly branded website
2) Set up and deliver new social media strategy
3) Set up and deliver local sponsorship programme

Breakthrough goal: Develop and empower the sales team

'How to' goals:
1) Recruit three new sales people
1) Agree roles and responsibilities, and job descriptions for everyone
3) Create and deliver a performance appraisal and training programme

Once you have set your goals, you will need to create a process to ensure they remain at the forefront of your mind, and that of your team's. You may have your goals displayed visually in your office, next to your Vision Orbit (discussed in Quick Win #3) or have them talked about and reviewed at meetings.

However you do it, you must keep focusing upon your goals – they will not miraculously happen simply as a result of being written down. Remember, a goal is like a seed – it needs to be fed and watered in order to grow.

Quick Success

I help my business-owner clients create twelve-month breakthrough goals at the start of their mentoring programme. We make sure that these breakthrough goals are in line with their business vision and that they are SMART.

They are written up on a chart and put on the wall alongside their Vision Orbit. This keeps them at the forefront of their minds, and ensures that they do not get lost in the day-to-day rush.

At each session we make sure that day-to-day actions are aligned with the plan to achieve these goals. Each goal requires a tactical action plan to make it happen.

Keeping it simple in this way has resulted in my business-owner clients being able to achieve their breakthrough goals, and to do so far more quickly than they had ever imagined. This is proof that this method works, and it gives them the confidence to reach for more.

Quick Actions
Take time to write down your three most important breakthrough goals and break them down into three 'how to' goals.

Make them all SMART.

Put them up on the wall so you can see them every day.

Personalise them with photos or pictures as this makes them more memorable and engaging.

5: Value your time

'Make each day count in an important way for you.'

When you are busy at work, it can be easy for time to run away from you. How many times have you wondered where the day went? Because we are all creatures of habit, the way we use our time is influenced by our habits, be they good ones or bad ones.

Making each day count in some way is vital if you want to grow your business. In order for it to change, improve and grow, you will need to carve out some time from the day-to-day routine – something many business owners neglect to do.

This time could be spent on matters such as developing a business and financial strategy, creating sales and marketing plans, obtaining customer feedback, or putting systems and procedures in place.

Your day-to-day activities will need to align with the steps required to achieve your breakthrough goals and, ultimately, your vision (described in Quick Wins #3 and #4). If there is no conscious alignment, the danger is that any time you spend will be taking you further away from your goals, not closer.

Quick Questions
Are you spending enough of your valuable time working *on* your business, rather than in it?

If you had an extra half-day a week, what would you spend it on?

Are you aware of what wastes your time?

Quick Win

Effective time management starts with an attitude of respect for your time, and for the time of others. Time is precious to everyone – we are all the same. If you are disorganised, it can affect those relying on you, and vice versa.

Here are some ideas to try out:

Keep a time log to analyse where your time is going and become conscious of your use of it. Get your team to do the same. Is this time being spent on actions that are in line with your vision?

Think about how you can be leaner and more efficient in what you do – what are you doing which is a waste of time?

Set aside a dedicated period of time to work on your business: daily, weekly, or monthly.

Talk to those staff and customers who are inefficient or disorganised and discuss how to work more effectively together. Set clear guidelines and give feedback.

Likewise, learn from colleagues who are efficient and organised, and seek to replicate their best working practices.

Think about what you can outsource to experts – what shouldn't you be doing that could be done more quickly and effectively by somebody else? (More on this with Quick Win #47.)

Set up systems and procedures for everything.

Use focused power hours to get important things done.

Make a weekly plan and allocate time slots for reviewing emails or undertaking social media.

Quick Success

Alan runs a leadership and management training business and spends most of his time delivering training programmes and creating course materials.

As a sole trader, he was finding it difficult to find time to work on his business as well as in it. It was a common problem – he never seemed to be able to find time to make any changes, as he was always too busy delivering. Consequently, he felt that he wasn't really getting anywhere.

Alan felt that, having reached his mid-fifties, he was running out of time, and he wanted to create some leverage in his business to maximise the return on his time and expertise.

Alan was used to working on his own, describing himself as 'a bit of a control freak' and a 'perfectionist'. No one could do things quite as well as he could and he was loath to delegate. However, this resulted in him spending a lot of his time doing things that he was either not good at, or not passionate about.

During our coaching sessions, we spent some time defining what Alan wanted to achieve from his business over the next ten years. Once he had connected with this, Alan suddenly had a clear vision with a focused set of goals – he became aware of exactly how he was spending his time and how much of it was being wasted.

He realised that it was far more efficient to outsource his business marketing, to hire an administration assistant and to finally get his systems and procedures organised.

Alan now has the resources to focus and deliver to larger clients in his niche sector, as well as freeing enough time to start writing the book he had always promised himself he would write.

Quick Actions

Keep a time log for a month and review it at the end of the month.

Start making each day count by spending a 'Power Hour' on something important that will help to grow your business.

Choose one thing you are doing in your business that you shouldn't be and either delegate it or pay an expert to do it for you.

Have an office clearout.

Chapter Review

Quick Wins to Get On Track and Motivated

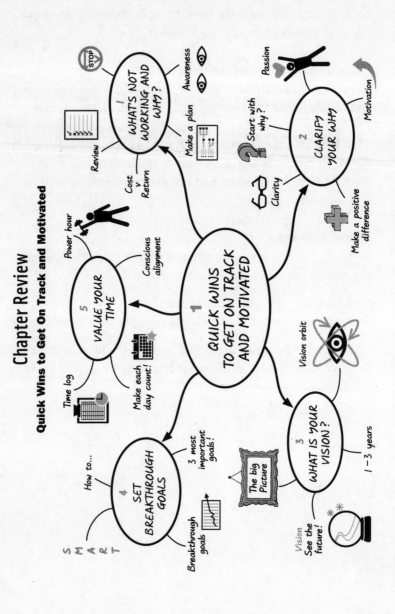

CHAPTER 2:
Quick Wins to Enhance Customer Retention and Profitability

6. Communicate regularly and review needs
7. Build a sales ladder and 'sell up'
8. Help customers to succeed
9. Accelerate trust and appreciation
10. Raise prices with value

6: Communicate regularly and review needs

*'Maintaining the connection and communication with
customers shows you continue to care.'*

When you acquire a new customer, there is usually a lot of
energy and enthusiasm at the outset. Your customer has
made the decision to use you because they believe that you
will provide the solution they are looking for. You are keen
to deliver and pleased because you have been chosen against
the competition. This is where the relationship starts.

There are many factors that will influence the length of
time that customer is active with you. The longer you can
keep a customer as an enthusiastic purchaser, the stronger
your business will be.

Here are some interesting statistics that show the main
reasons customers give for ceasing to do business with
a supplier:

1 per cent of customers die

3 per cent move out of the area

5 per cent are influenced away

9 per cent get a 'better deal'

14 per cent leave because of unresolved conflicts

68 per cent leave because of perceived indifference –
i.e. apathy or lack of communication on the part of
the supplier.

By nurturing your customers from the start and maintaining communication, you will avoid losing the two-thirds (or 68 per cent to be exact) who stop being your customers because of perceived indifference.

Quick Questions

How many of your past customers have you been in touch with recently?

Who has bought in the past but is not at the moment? Do you know why?

Quick Win

The need to communicate

Continuing to communicate with your customers after they have finished doing business with you will ensure that your customers know you care. It will also leave the door open for future business.

The need to review needs

Your customers' needs will probably change over time. The reason a person became a customer in the first place may not be the same reason for them continuing to buy from you now.

Taking the time to understand your existing customers' changing needs will ensure that you are there with the solutions before they think of using anyone else. It is important that you keep talking to your customers as they can be a great source of information for you.

Taking your existing customers' business for granted without reviewing their needs is risky. Do they know about the full range of products and services you offer? If not, they could be attracted elsewhere if someone new comes along with an answer to a problem you didn't even know about.

I recently stopped using a customer relationship management (CRM) system we had been paying for and using for years. I had been planning to stop using it for at least six months prior to cancelling our contract. When I spoke to the business owner, he was sorry that he hadn't realised the service wasn't working for us as well as it could have been. Many things had changed in our business that he was unaware of, but by the time I made the call to cancel, it was too late to put it right. I wasn't complaining; I was out.

Your regular communication system could include:

Monthly bulletin with useful tips and information

Connecting on Facebook or LinkedIn

New product or service alerts

An invite to a special event

A Christmas card

An invitation to an outside event, such as a golf day or a day at the races

Useful information or learning opportunity

A reminder of a renewal date or service that is due

A regular review meeting.

You will need to decide what you want to achieve and design your communication system accordingly. It will depend on the type of business you are in and the interests of your customers.

A well-organised customer-relationship management system will help to make this whole process easier for you to implement and manage on an ongoing basis.

Elements of a customer review meeting

The right approach

It is important to use a customer review opportunity to build on your existing relationship. Your customers are busy like you and will need to be given a good reason to spend the time reviewing their needs with you. So your approach is key.

Just inviting your customer for a long lunch without setting up the reason for that lunch is likely to waste both your time and theirs. You have to give them a reason to meet you. The review meeting could be set up as a form of regular, free consultancy, where you follow a distinct structure looking at the past and present before looking forward to the future.

The right time

It is a good idea to set up the expectation of a customer review meeting with every new customer. It could become part of the commitment you offer to your customers when you start your business relationship with them.

Your customer review meetings need to be scheduled for a time that anticipates the potentially changing needs of your customers. This might be at the end of their financial year or the end of the calendar year. It may be annually or six-monthly. It might be seasonally – in any case, the time needs to be appropriate for both parties.

The right preparation

To successfully review your customers' needs, you will need to have full details of their purchasing history. You can anticipate some future needs based on past patterns.

Taking the time to find out a little about their marketplace and industry also helps in predicting future needs; indeed, ones they themselves might not yet be aware of. You will need to have a list available of the work you have completed for them.

The right questions

Your customer review will need an outcome and an action plan, both of which can be achieved with the right questions guiding the review.

Customer review questions

What do you want to achieve at our review meeting?

How happy or satisfied have you been with the service/product we have provided for you over this period?

What, if anything, could we improve on?

In terms of the service we offer, what is most important to you?

What are some of the problems you anticipate might need solving over the next year?

What is your focus for the next six/twelve months?

What are your priorities?

How could we help you over the next twelve months?

An action plan and new proposal
It is important to have an agreed action plan at the end of the review, which could be confirmed by a review proposal for future business.

Quick Success
The company that we have been outsourcing our social media to holds a regular review meeting with us every six weeks. They set aside an hour and a half to discuss results and plan their ongoing strategy. This enables them to pick up on any changing needs we have, get important feedback and educate us so that we can support the process. They always prepare well for these meetings and have all the necessary facts and figures to hand.

We get all of our questions answered and go away feeling positive. These review meetings ensure their continued and developing business with us and build our confidence in their service.

We are also on their newsletter list and receive regular social media tips and ideas; we are connected on LinkedIn and Facebook too. I have also been asked to be a guest blogger on their regular communication with their customers.

Our relationship was quickly and firmly established as a result of these regular communication and review meetings.

Quick Actions

Set up a series of review meetings with relevant existing customers.

Set up a communication system to stay in touch with existing and past customers.

SALES LADDER

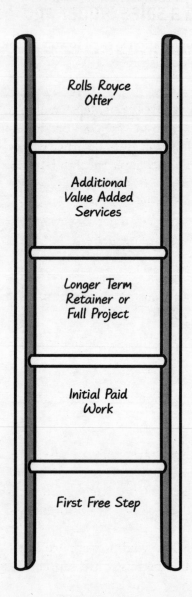

Rolls Royce
Offer

Additional
Value Added
Services

Longer Term
Retainer or
Full Project

Initial Paid
Work

First Free Step

7: Build a sales ladder and 'sell up'

'Taking one small step at a time makes the climb to the top far easier.'

A sales ladder is a series of steps created to enable your customer to buy from you comfortably and easily. The easy steps enable you to build trust with your customer and to gradually encourage them to buy more from you.

It is a way of presenting what you are offering in stages, in order to help your customer engage with you at a pace and price that is right for them.

Quick Questions

What steps does a customer need to take to engage with and buy from you?

Do you have an easy first engagement step?

Quick Win

Your sales ladder should be something like this:

First free step

Your sales ladder starts with an easy, free step to build trust in the relationship. This could be anything from a review of an element of your potential customer's business, to a health check or a brainstorming session.

This free step is also your first opportunity to have a sales conversation. During this conversation, you will have the opportunity to understand your client's needs, and to help educate them to make an informed decision about taking the next step up your sales ladder.

Initial piece of paid work

The second rung of your ladder should be a piece of paid work in order to prepare your customer for the next stage of the process. It could be a Discovery Workshop to enable full scoping of a bigger project, a fuller review of needs, or a plan of action to solve a particular problem.

This initial piece of paid work is your customer's first commitment. From this you can prove your value and build more trust.

Longer-term retainer or full project

The next rung of the ladder involves commitment to a longer-term plan. It could be an ongoing retainer for a certain number of days per month, a full project implementation, or a complete package of client services.

Additional value-added services

Further rungs up the ladder may involve adding additional services such as a maintenance or service contract, or a pay-as-you-go package that the customer only has access to after making a longer term commitment.

Top price, top value

At the top of your sales ladder is your 'Rolls Royce' offering. This is your best offering, your top price and top value package. Add in as much additional value as you can. This level might involve some personal time with you as the director of the company.

This offering can be aimed at customers who want to take the 'fast track' – they have the budget and want the benefits now, jumping straight from the first rung of the sales ladder.

Design your own ladder

Take the sales ladder concept and design one specifically to suit your business. You may have a lower price option which requires commitment from the customer over a longer period of time, or a higher priced option for a shorter-term commitment. Give your customers a choice.

'Sell up' and sell more

To be able to 'sell up' – getting your customers to purchase services from higher up the sales ladder – and therefore sell more to your customers, you need to have worked through how your offering is structured, what you want your customer to buy from you and at what stage in the buying process it will be offered.

Quick Success

A CRM company delivers an initial education workshop as a free first step on their sales ladder. This leads to step two, which is a paid-for Discovery Workshop to scope the project more fully. Step three is full commitment to the project implementation and step four is a series of training workshops to enable the team and the company to get the best out of their CRM system.

A PR and social media company delivers an initial free consultation to establish their client's social media and PR goals. During this time, they educate the customer about what can be achieved with the right strategy. The next rung of the ladder is an initial commitment to a bespoke strategy-planning session and a three-month implementation plan. This then moves on to a longer-term retainer with built-in monthly review meetings. They also have a 'Rolls Royce' offering that incorporates consultancy from the top creative director in the company.

A cash and credit control company delivers a confidential cash flow health check as their first free step. This leads to a Quick Win piece of work to secure outstanding debts, and then on to a paid piece of work to set up systems and management reporting procedures, and to train the team. The fourth rung of the ladder is a retained monthly meeting to deliver management information and provide consultancy services. The 'Rolls Royce' offering is the complete outsourced service.

Quick Actions
Design your own sales ladder.

Create a 'Rolls Royce' package at top price, adding in as much highly perceived value as you can.

Ask more customers to climb up the ladder.

8: Help customers to succeed

*'Help your customers achieve what they want and
you will receive what you want.'*

The more success you can help your customers to achieve, the more likely it is that they will continue doing business with you. So, if you want to retain your clients and increase their spend, focus on helping them to reach their goals and outcomes.

Being able to help your customers succeed starts with understanding their needs and creating suitable strategies and solutions to meet those needs.

The desire to help your customers succeed is as much an attitude of mind as it is a set of actions. If you are clearly focused upon your customers' success, they will pick up on that and reward you accordingly.

Think of the supplier who is purely focused on getting paid, compared to the one who is excited about delivering results for you and helping you to achieve your goals. Which are you more likely to continue to do business with? Our intentions can be very powerful, especially when clearly set out at the start, and delivered on with passion.

You may need to manage your clients' expectations in order to help them to succeed. We all have clients who don't help themselves get results and who think that simply by agreeing to our services, we will make it happen for them. It is important to define expectations, and a way of working that will facilitate success.

You may have to nip problems in the bud before they grow, and brief your clients on things they can do to enhance the results they receive from your services.

Quick Questions

What is the greatest success you have achieved for one of your clients?

What is your best intention for your clients?

Do you have a way of working that helps your clients get the best results from the service you offer?

Quick Win

How to help your clients succeed

- Set clear expectations from the start and manage those expectations

- Educate and train where necessary

- Agree a way of working that will ensure your work is completed as efficiently and as effectively as possible

- Set up a feedback system to deal with any problems before they get in the way

- Discuss your clients' success to them

- Be clear on what you require from your clients

- Make your systems easy and simple to follow

- Communicate clearly.

Quick Success

I have to be very clear when working in a mentoring or training capacity that before even starting the process, I want to agree a scope of work with clear outcomes. Defining these outcomes at the outset ensures clarity for both the client and for me, so that we both know what we are aiming for and what success 'looks like'. Having worked with many business owners over the years, I have seen many succeed as a result of the mentoring process, but I have also experienced those that have not worked so well.

The ones that didn't work so well tended to be those where clients insisted on doing their own thing, left big gaps between sessions, or tried to fast-track the process by attempting too much in too short a time period.

If a business owner commits to mentoring but then fails to allocate time, prepare properly, or follow through on their actions, it can be very hard to achieve the desired results. It also makes it difficult for the mentor to retain a connection with the business.

I find the best way to start the process is to explain the methodology that I find works best from experience, then agree some ways of working whilst allowing for flexibility. This is an excellent way of ensuring that the client commits to the process, and at the same time avoids any rigidity.

A dynamic business requires flexibility since there will always be changes over time that don't always fit with the initial plan on paper.

To work well, mentoring and training must help practical day-to-day delivery, as well as longer-term planning. For their part, business owners need to be committed and focused, and be prepared to allocate time to work on the agreed actions for their businesses.

A mentor should be a guide and an inspiration to the business owner, somebody who provides structure to their thinking whilst maintaining accountability for their actions. They are similar in a way to a fitness coach – if you want to get fit, you have to take regular exercise, and if you want to grow your business, you have to commit to taking the action to make it happen.

I review my clients' successes at the start of every mentoring session – this provides the opportunity for reflection, learning and praise. It is a very important part of the journey, creating the positive energy necessary to simulate more of the same. (Read more about this in Quick Win #50.)

Quick Actions
Set up a way of working that will ensure your clients succeed.

Ask your clients about their successes.

9: Accelerate trust and appreciation

*'Saying "thank you" for all the little things is a
big thing for the receiver.'*

A trusting relationship develops when your customers feel
connected with you as a person and confident that you
have their best interests at heart. You will then be their first
choice when they have a relevant problem that needs
solving. Trust is built up over time and through experience.

If you maintain a level of service that delivers what you
have promised, does what you say you are going to do,
and leaves your customer fully satisfied, then it will be
easy to build trust. Trust is about integrity and values – it
matters deeply and is very personal.

Trusting relationships form the backbone of successful
businesses. In a world where there is usually almost too
much choice, people will always support those whom they
trust, since this builds security.

If customers trust you, they will listen to your advice,
make decisions based on your suggestions and not question your prices . . . or at least, not as much as they would
if they were unsure about you! Building trusting relationships helps to retain existing customers, gain new ones
and increase referrals.

However, in the same way as you can build trust with

proper attention to detail, trust can also be broken in an instant. For example, forgetting to send out a proposal or to follow up by telephone when you have promised to do so, a sharp word when tired or stressed, or forgetting your customer's name – these are all silly mistakes that can affect customers' belief in you and your service.

All of our customers can provide learning opportunities. As well as paying us, they offer us the chance to learn and grow as we work with them. It is good to recognise that and be thankful for it. It is my belief that whenever you show appreciation for what you get in your life, it will keep on coming. So, by appreciating the opportunity to work with your customers, you will accelerate the 'flow'.

Quick Questions

How much trust have you built up with your clients?

How do you know they trust you?

Quick Win

How to accelerate trust

- Value the business your customers are giving you

- See the best in them and their business

- Say 'thank you' to them for choosing to work with you

- If you see a business opportunity for your customers, put them in touch

- Ask questions and listen carefully to what they want

- Be personal and remember the important details in their lives

- Show you understand what matters to them

- Be honest, even if it means that you do not sell your services

- Give something away for free – ideas, advice or education

- Deliver whatever you promise and do it well

- Take a real sense of pride in your work

- Let people know early on if, for any reason, you cannot deliver

- Always do the best you can

- Contact your customers personally if there is a problem

- Focus on the results that matter to them

- Be thankful for the opportunity to learn from the customers you work with

- Do something extra special for them from time to time – send them a relevant article that relates to their business, a book that you think will help them with something they are struggling with, or information about some equipment or facilities they are considering

- Be conscious of the trust you already have and are continuing to build with your customers. Notice the signs. Work harder to both build it and maintain it. It will all be worth it.

Quick Success

I look forward to every mentoring session I have with my clients. They are a joy, even when challenging . . . and most are fun too! The best and most successful relationship I have is with a team of directors whom I have been mentoring for over three years.

They valued the mentoring so much that they continued even when they went through a bad patch and didn't draw salaries for a few months. I am very grateful for that and they have reaped the rewards for that commitment. They are now very profitable, and have won a number of prestigious business awards.

Quick Actions

Think of all the clients you have had and what you have learnt from them.

Make a list of everything in your business that you appreciate.

10: Raise prices with value

'Only when you raise the value, can you then raise the price.'

Higher prices mean higher profit margins, right? However, people do not buy on price alone, and raising prices can have other implications for your business. On the one hand, raising your prices may provide you with more resources, enabling you to add more value to your service and therefore to stand out from the crowd. But higher prices will often result in you losing the bottom end of your customer base.

You may want to lose this bottom end because it contains low-priced jobs that take time and effort to service. In this case, raising prices becomes a conscious strategy for subtly disengaging with unprofitable, time-consuming customers.

The effect on your customer depends upon their sensitivity to price rises – some may barely notice. Think about your local restaurant: if they raised the price of your favourite main course dish from £10.50 to £11.75, would you stop ordering it?

However, if you are going to raise your prices, it is important to do it in the right way and at the right time. Your loyal, regular customers will need advance warning to ensure they are not taken by surprise.

If you can show your customers that you have raised your game as well as your prices, and are now offering more value than you were before, it will make it easier for them to accept any changes. Customers rarely buy on price alone but, if they do, they often don't receive the value they had anticipated.

Quick Questions
How do your prices reflect the value you offer?

Could you raise your prices?

Quick Win
How and when you raise your prices will depend upon the nature of your business.

How to raise your prices
When putting a pricing strategy together, make sure you consider both the market conditions and your competition. Decide what it is that you want to achieve with your price rises.

Consider the impact of financial year-ends to ensure that any price increases can be factored into upcoming budgets – make it as easy as possible for your existing customers to adapt to your price increases. A new calendar year, or the start of your financial year, can be good times to move forward with price increases, as can after particular sales periods, the introduction of new stock lines or refurbishments.

Consider the additional value you are able to offer to justify your price rises and make sure you communicate this to your customers.

Packaging to increase revenue and value
Packaging your products or services means grouping them together to enable you to sell more, and so that your customer enjoys greater value for money.

Packaging in this manner will increase the amount your customer spends with you, without having to raise your prices.

Packaging will enable you to sell more by:

- Promoting a higher perceived value
- Automatically allowing you to up-sell without having to ask for it
- Creating the opportunity to work with your customer over a longer time period
- Helping to move slow-moving stock by attaching it to more popular new stock.

Here are some examples of how companies package their products that you might recognise:

An all-inclusive holiday where the customer pays one quoted price and receives their flights, accommodation, food, drink and other benefits such as the use of sports facilities, all bundled together in an attractive package.

A fast-food restaurant that offers a 'meal deal', where you receive the burger of your choice, fries and a drink for a set price.

A training company that offers a complete programme of modular sessions that link together.

A book shop offering you a 'buy both together' price for the book you have requested and a second, related book.

A hotel that offers special weekend breaks inclusive of dinner, bed and breakfast.

Restaurants that offer special set menus to encourage people to dine at quieter times.

Quick Success

Steve, a marketing consultant, wanted to raise his game and work with bigger, more profitable clients. A lot of the smaller clients he was attracting had tight budgets and were very time- and effort-intensive. Steve wanted to reduce his client portfolio whilst increasing his revenues and profitability.

He decided to raise his prices to reflect the change in the clients he was now targeting. He thought about the problems and needs of these clients and adjusted his offering accordingly, including a strategic marketing consultancy service backed up by a delivery team to execute agreed plans.

He even started charging a fee for the initial exploratory step on his sales ladder, which he used to give away for nothing. (See Quick Win #7.)

The result was that as soon as his focus changed, his business changed. He is now working with clients who have the budgets to spend outsourcing their marketing activities to Steve's team, and is able to achieve a higher daily rate for his strategic marketing consultancy.

Quick Actions

Consider where you could charge more for what you offer and try it.

Could you achieve more revenue through packaging your products and services, giving more to get customers spending a bit more?

Chapter Review

Quick Wins to Enhance Customer Retention and Profitability

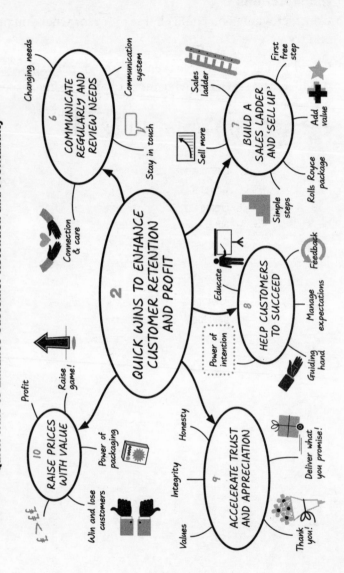

CHAPTER 3:
Quick Wins to Attract Top-quality Leads

11. Define your ideal customer
12. Target the best niche
13. Create the perfect prospecting list
14. Put the right bait on your hook
15. Focus your networking
16. Develop alliance and joint-venture partners
17. Work your black book
18. Ask for referrals and recommendations
19. Develop an opportunity radar
20. Use special offers and incentives

11: Define your ideal customer

'Your best customers are usually your biggest fans.'

Defining your 'ideal customer' means clarifying the people, or businesses, most likely to be willing to buy your product or service.

What makes a customer ideal?

- They already want what you are selling

- They are willing to pay for it

- There are a number of them in the market

- You know how to access them

- You enjoy working with them

- You find it easy to sell them your product or service.

Quick Questions
How many 'ideal customers' have you attracted to your business to date?

Do you want more?

Quick Win
When working with my mentoring clients, I use the following structure to help them define their 'ideal customers':

Business type: sector/industry/market niche

Person: characteristics/personality/age

Size: number of employees/turnover

Location: geographic

Values: what is important to them?

Problems: that your product or service could resolve

Needs: that your solution could fulfil.

Knowing who it is you are targeting will greatly influence how you communicate your product or service to them. Targeted marketing and sales activities will save you a great deal of wasted time and effort, preventing you from 'fishing in the wrong pond'.

Quick Success
Colin, the director of a company distributing and manufacturing wheels and castors, wanted to increase his number of 'ideal customers'.

Colin was a young, dynamic entrepreneur with aspirations to become a market leader in his niche. Roughly 50 per cent of his sales were online or through distributors – these were low margin/high volume sales. Colin wanted to concentrate his personal sales time on increasing the number of higher margin/lower volume customers.

Colin and I spent some time defining his 'ideal customer', which helped him to identify two brand-new targets for his products. He delegated the task of researching these potential new target sectors to his team. They managed to uncover a new set of needs, which they and Colin would not have thought of from the outset.

By understanding these needs, Colin was able to tailor his sales and marketing message accordingly. He has since opened two big new accounts with 'ideal customers', and is now well on his way to reaching his ambitious sales targets.

Quick Actions

Jot down a description of your ideal target customer.

Identify the customers in your marketplace which most closely fit this description.

Approach these potential customers, asking open-ended questions to establish their particular needs.

Use these needs as the foundation for your sales and marketing strategy.

12: Target the best niche

'Master your niche and become a celebrity.'

A niche is generally thought of as a specific customer, group or sector. For example, personal fitness training for busy corporate executives, raising finance for growing biotech companies, or business mentoring for dentists' practices.

Many business owners are afraid to concentrate upon a particular niche in case it limits them. However, the opposite is usually the case.

'The eagle that chases two rabbits catches neither.'
– African proverb

Concentrating on a niche will enable you to focus and be the best you can be for a smaller portion of the market. Additionally, you will become known as the expert for that particular sub-section – experts are regarded as people who can be trusted, and trust accelerates opportunities.

Once you are clear about your niche, you will find it a lot easier to explain to people what you do. People will also find it easier to remember and refer you. Your marketing efforts will become concentrated, and are likely to have more impact.

Quick Questions
Do you have a niche target customer group you could serve as the expert?

Which niche do you have the most experience and passion for?

Quick Win
Selecting a niche does need a lot of thought as it will be the foundation upon which your marketing strategy is built. Hence, you will need to do your market and customer research.

Niche checklist

- Do you know a group of people/businesses with a common problem that you can solve?

- Do they have the ability and willingness to pay?

- Is there a large enough number to support your business?

- Are they easy to track down and communicate with?

- Do you have the experience and the expertise for this niche?

- Are there others operating within that niche?

- If so, could you do it better?

- If you have no competition, could you be the first?

Once you have selected your niche, you can start to promote yourself as the relevant expert. Your aim is to become 'famous' for your expertise in this particular niche. Get people to talk about you, recommend you to others, and be inspired to buy your services.

Quick Success

When Tim and Jayne were contemplating the best way to build their business development, coaching and training business, they realised that they already had a strong niche. All their experience had been in the health industry, working with all sizes of businesses, from small to large corporates, and with all subjects, from humans to animals.

They had worked with suppliers, both in the UK and Europe, to bridge the customer communication gap between large pharmaceutical companies, the health practices they served and the end-user customer. Their passion for making a difference was health-related.

At first they were afraid to focus in case they missed out on other business opportunities. However, they soon realised they could stand out as trusted experts if they used their experience and case studies to their marketing advantage.

This decision meant changing the more generic marketing collateral they were just about to invest in.

There is no doubt in their minds that this was the right decision. If they hadn't claimed this space in the market, they would simply have got lost in the crowd.

Quick Actions

Choose a niche for your business by researching its viability.

Set out a plan of action to be seen as the expert in that niche.

13: Create the perfect prospecting list

*'Get me to raise my hand and let you know I am the
right prospect for your list.'*

A prospecting list is essential for marketing purposes, whether by email, newsletter or telesales. It is best to build these lists yourself. The better your list is, the more likely you are to convert leads into customers.

The best prospecting list is one that has been opted into by the potential customers in your chosen market.

If someone agrees to opt into your list, they will have metaphorically raised their hand. Your list will contain the names, addresses and contact details of people who have agreed to, or asked to be contacted by you.

They could be online contacts who have ticked a box on one of your website forms saying that they would like to receive a free monthly newsletter, report or special promotion. Alternatively, they may have handed you a business card at a networking event or after a talk, and asked to receive your information.

Building your own list ensures that every name represents somebody who has demonstrated an interest in what you do, or what you offer. Hence, it is cost-effective and targeted.

Quick Questions

Review your prospecting list – is it targeted or vague?

Do you have a relationship with the people on your list?

Quick Win

To attract people to your list, you will require something of value to inspire them.

How to build your opt-in list

- Put the 'right bait on your hook' before you go fishing (more of this in Quick Win #14)

- Offer something free as an opt-in hook: a report, sample, tips sheet, company health check, consultation – anything which would motivate those in your target market

- Integrate these opt-in hooks into each of your channels to market in the appropriate way

- Link these opt-in opportunities to an e-communication tool, such as MailChimp or Constant Contact, which will enable you to communicate with your prospecting list

- If your current prospecting list is cluttered with recipients who haven't opened any of your newsletters or mailings for over a year, they are not worth having – do not be afraid to cut targets.

An opt-in prospecting list is different from a target list that would be prepared for telemarketing.

How to build your telemarketing prospecting list

- If you are building a list for a telemarketing campaign, begin by researching the companies that operate within your niche

- Use online forensic tools to discover who has visited your website, and analyse which pages they have clicked on

- Use your newsletter opt-in list and those who have engaged with you through social media, as these are the people you already have a relationship with.

It is possible to buy in focused data from outside sources, such as list brokers, who will put targets together to fulfil your specific criteria. This data will not be as good as those you have already built a relationship with but, with a good telemarketing approach, the engagement can still be made.

Building good-quality prospecting lists are the best way to ensure a solid foundation from which to market your business. The right list will save you hours of wasted marketing budget.

Quick Success

Anne-Marie and Steve, the directors of a PR and social media company, regularly use a telephone appointment-making service to arrange meetings with good-quality prospective clients.

Having tested a variety of companies and approaches, they have found their greatest success has been when they have used very focused, pre-qualified prospecting lists that pass the 'ideal client' test (see Quick Win #11).

They have expertise in a number of niche areas (see Quick Win #12), pharmaceutical and automotive being two of their strongest, so their list building is directed towards building higher-quality engagement with those particular markets.

Their prospect-finding activities have been measurably more effective since working from lists of business owners who have raised their hands, engaged through website visits and social media, or who have been properly researched and targeted.

They are now winning more new clients in the markets they can best serve.

Quick Actions

If you have an existing prospecting list, make sure it is up to date – if not, prune it.

If you are considering a telemarketing campaign for the first time, put together a small list of good-quality prospects to test the process.

14: Put the right bait on your hook

'Hungry fish are attracted by food; hungry buyers are attracted by solutions.'

To attract the right business owners to your prospecting list, you will need to entice them with something that is worth them giving you their contact details or taking the first step to buy from you.

If you fully understand your typical target clients' problems and needs, it will be easy for you to decide on the right bait for your hook.

Great bait for the right prospects can range from free downloadable reports, to free monthly tips sheets and apps. They can also include free webinars, consultations, business health checks, seminars, videos or talks. It may even be a free book!

The bait you use will need to be designed to give your prospects information that they will value highly. It must promise to solve a problem, ease the hunger pain, or point towards a particular solution.

For some businesses, education can be the vital first step in their sales process. Many buyers spend some time researching for information before they are ready to commit to a supplier.

They may have downloaded your free report, received your newsletter, watched your videos, or linked with you on social media for years before they contact you as a buyer.

Giving away some of your expertise builds trust in your service.

I recently started work with a business mentoring client who contacted me five years after meeting me at an event. I had offered her the opportunity to receive my monthly sales and marketing tips and ideas as a way of staying in touch. She called me out of the blue and it was as if we had a relationship already. My tips over the years had built her trust in my knowledge and she was at the point where she was ready to buy more.

Quick Questions
What bait do you have to attract hungry prospects for your service?

What do you give away in return for their contact details?

Quick Win
Here are some examples of bait that business owners have used to attract their prospects:

A finance director who specialises in raising finance for business ventures offers a free report called 'How to raise finance for your business venture.'

An estate agent offers a free monthly property industry update with buying and selling tips and advice.

A consultant who specialises in buying and selling businesses offers a talk and a report entitled 'How much is your business worth?'

A social media company offers a selection of free reports, videos and talks with a host of simple practical tips to make social media work.

I have an app called Heart of Biz, which sends you one of my daily inspirations every morning, as well as a number of very useful networking tools.

(You can download the Heart of Biz app from the App Store or the Play Store for Android. It gives you some useful networking tools and information about events.)

How to bait your hook

Develop a title for your free report, newsletter, talk or video that promises a benefit and suggests important learning.

Create some lead generation messages that market your bait, which you can communicate to your customers.

You will need to put these lead generation messages in places where your 'hungry crowd' is most likely to be. Your lead generation messages will be the relevant link to get the bait.

Places where you can market your bait

LinkedIn groups

Online discussion forums

Facebook

Twitter

Google Plus

Professional and industry associations

Specialist magazines or websites

Networking groups – online and offline

Google adverts

On your own website

Via your alliance or joint-venture partners email list.

Quick Success

Julia, who runs a successful social media company, constantly 'baits her hook' in order to build and maintain her prospecting list. She has developed a series of quick video tips that give away useful information about how to make the most of LinkedIn, Twitter and Facebook.

She also has a great social media blog on which she promotes the videos, and has just written a book with free chapters that she gives away as 'tasters'.

Julia goes around the country giving short practical talks on the power of social media, offering her quick tips as a way of maintaining and building the relationship with her audience.

Her marketing strategy is all about education. She keeps everything simple – giving away tasters at the outset to attract hand-raisers (i.e. those who could be in the market for her service) and then continuing to offer just enough to maintain and build those relationships until customers are ready to buy.

Being an expert in social media, Julia uses that expertise to market her bait. The result has been a huge following and a consistent supply of new clients.

She 'walks the talk' and gives a lot away in order to gain the trust of potential customers.

Quick Actions

Set aside some time to create your own bait, and a strategy to use it to build your following.

Offer your bait wherever you go.

Measure your success by the numbers on your list.

15: Focus your networking

'The best relationships in business produce the best results, so work your relationships.'

Networking develops business contacts and relationships that enable you to expand your business. It also increases your knowledge and builds your profile in the community.

It can be short- or long-term – you may see immediate returns, or you might not see a return from it for months or years. My own experience of networking has been extremely positive; I have usually made at least one worthwhile business contact at every networking event that I have ever attended.

Remember, though, that this is a two-way process – it is about giving as well as receiving. As you meet new people and build up your contacts, you will find yourself able to refer or recommend people whose services you have used yourself.

There are so many different types of networking events to choose from that there will be one to suit everyone's needs. If you are an early riser, a breakfast meeting might suit; short of time, and a one-hour lunch event could be preferable; prefer a more formalised environment, and a longer evening event might be best. There are many different formats: speaker sessions, discussion groups, business referrals, speed networking events . . . and so on.

The most important thing is to choose the networking event that is most suitable for you and the target audience you are looking for. Our Heart of Biz app has details of the different kinds of networking events available for ambitious business owners.

Quick Questions

What do you want your networking to achieve?

Which events do you attend that enable you to meet potential clients or alliances?

Quick Win

Before you go networking, first establish what you want to achieve – for example, who would be your ideal customer, how you will promote yourself and what will your follow-up method be?

Here are some top tips:

- Focus on relationship building, not selling

- Be interested in other people's businesses and their needs

- Listen for challenges that you might be able to help with, or that you can refer on to others

- Speak to as many people as you can – mix and mingle

- If you are invited to speak for a few minutes about who you are and what you do, know your USPs and have a short pre-prepared one-minute introduction (see below for a structure to follow)

- Be clear about what you are looking for in terms of new business – the more specific you can be, the better (see Quick Win #12)

- Take plenty of business cards with you (I know this is obvious but many people don't!)

- Note down the date and name of the networking event on the business cards you collect. I also frequently jot down something distinctive about a person's features or clothing on the back of their business card, to help me remember them afterwards

- Follow up immediately afterwards with a brief email, letter or invitation to connect on a networking site (such as LinkedIn) – don't wait or you will forget!

- Build up a few networking events that you like and attend them on a regular basis for a while – this will make it easier to build stronger relationships and trust

- Review your successes. How many new contacts have ultimately led to more business?

Quick Success

I have shared the following structure for short speeches with many of my clients over the years. It helps them to prepare what to say about their business in one minute, in order to inspire fellow networkers. Using a structure to prepare for your speech will make it easier to talk naturally and get your key message across.

Here is an example we created for a tele-appointment making company, which worked very well for them:

Who are you, what do you do, and for whom?
I am Peter Smith, from Telemarketing Success based in Oxford. We specialise in making warm sales appointments with potential clients for business coaches, advisers and consultants.

What big problem do you solve for your clients?
We solve the problem coaches and consultants have with 'feast and famine' by providing them with a consistent pipeline of sales leads.

What is special about the way you work with clients?
We are different from most telemarketing companies in the sense that we only charge our clients for the successful appointments we make for them. This is after running a test campaign to ensure we can achieve results in their defined market.

What do your clients value most about your service?
Our clients value the fact that we do the hard work of opening doors, leaving them free to concentrate on what they are good at. They also all appreciate our efficient weekly reporting and feedback system.

What results have you achieved?
We regularly provide the coaches and consultants that use us with six good appointments a month, and most win at least one in three.

[Note: it is important in a pitch to quote specific results in financial terms or to give an example of success such as profitability, saving money, achieving an important outcome, etc.]

What is your first step to engage with a client?

We start with an initial half-hour telephone consultation to discuss what the client does, who they target, the appointments they want and how our process works.

Call to action

If you are interested in finding out more please give me your card and we will contact you to arrange a convenient time to talk.

Quick Actions

Practise and fine-tune until you are happy with your short networking speeches.

Make a commitment to attend at least two good networking events a month.

Create a follow-up system and stick to it.

16: Develop alliance and joint-venture partners

'Together we are stronger.'

Alliances or joint ventures are extremely effective ways to gain access to potential new customers. Provided they are clearly defined from the outset and properly implemented by both parties, they are win-win-win for all involved, including the most important person, the customer.

Alliances

Alliances seek to harness the goodwill and strong customer relationships that other businesses have already established with prime prospects for your product or service.

If you form a relationship with a business that is not in direct competition with you, but which sells to the same people as you, you could both be of potential benefit to each other.

A business with which you might form an alliance relationship will be selling something that goes before, alongside or after your product or service.

Here are some examples of successful alliances:

- A business consultant forming an alliance relationship with an accountant or a solicitor

- A plumber forming an alliance relationship with an electrician or building company

- A printing company forming an alliance relationship with a website or a marketing company.

Since your alliance partner already has a relationship with their customers, they can provide you with a solid and trusted foundation.

If an alliance partner is willing to recommend your services to their customers, it provides you with free marketing. In return, you may recommend their products or service to your customers.

Joint ventures

A joint venture is when you are given permission to access another business's customers directly. Joint-venture marketing is the process of marketing to customers of complementary businesses. It involves your partner endorsing your product or service through their customer database, in return for the same, or for an agreed commission on sales made.

Here are some examples of useful joint ventures:

- A hair salon sharing customers with a gym, beauty salon, nail bar or nutritional therapist

- A hotel sharing customers with appropriate restaurants, bars, tourist attractions or theatres.

Quick Question

Who already sells to the customers you want to reach?

Try to think laterally, or take note of existing alliance relationships that you come across online, in magazines or in specialist publications.

Quick Win

Use the following steps to create alliances:

1. Make a list of potential alliances in your marketplace. Think about what you have to offer as an alliance partner – what makes your offer unique and attractive? Which joint-venture relationships could complement your offering?

2. Choose a selection of companies to contact. Define your common goals – write them down at the outset so that both parties are clear and in agreement.

3. Explore and brainstorm the best ways of working together to achieve these goals – alliances, joint ventures or affiliates.

4. Ask the other party what they would need to know about your service to feel confident enough to recommend you or undertake a joint venture with you.

5. Agree the rewards system – how you will measure and review.

6. Agree the required input from both parties to progress the plan; i.e. marketing collateral, time, etc.

Quick Success

Almost ten years ago, a not-for-profit group called parkrun began organising a free, weekly 5km timed run, which took place at 9 a.m. every Saturday morning in Bushy Park, Teddington. The concept spread, and now there are around 300 events across the UK, and as far afield as Russia, South Africa and Australia, with each parkrun attracting anything from fifty to over 1,000 runners.

Being a keen runner myself, I am a regular participant at the Abingdon parkrun, as well as a 'tourist' (official parkrun terminology here!) at other parkruns around the country. Everybody is encouraged (but not required) to help out by volunteering, and after each run, your position and time is displayed on your particular parkrun's website. However, the focus of parkrun is in encouraging people to exercise, hence free T-shirts are given out for completing a number of runs: 10 (juniors only), 50, 100 and 250.

In Abingdon, Café Java quickly realised the appeal of parkrun, and became the coffee shop of choice for Abingdon parkrunners. They offer a special discount to those who present a parkrun barcode, and receive weekly promotions before every event as the suggested place to meet up over a coffee and breakfast after the run.

The result is that Café Java now has a queue right across the market square from 9.30 a.m. every Saturday morning, and has become the meeting place of choice for local runners.

Quick Actions

Think of three potential alliances for your business and establish contact with them for an exploratory conversation.

Consider who you could set up a win-win-win joint venture with.

17: Work your black book

'Who you already know may know who you need to know.'

Throughout your business life, you will no doubt have already built up a number of relationships and contacts. You may or may not have kept in touch with these people, but you will have had a business relationship with them at some point in the past. They represent your 'black book'.

The reality is that it can be hard to keep up with those contacts who are not on your day-to-day radar. However, it is essential to try to maintain these positive relationships as much as possible, since you never know when you might be able to help each other. Social media outlets such as LinkedIn make it much easier now to keep in touch with contacts and to find out where they are and what they are doing.

Why might you need to work your black book?

- You require an introduction to an alliance or a potential joint-venture partner, and one of your black book contacts might know them, or is in contact with someone who knows them

- You are starting a new business venture, or launching a new product, which you need to publicise and which could be of interest or value to your contacts

- You are building a business and would like to get introductions to potential new clients.

The 'Six Degrees of Separation' rule suggests that, through our network, we are only ever six steps away from getting in touch with the relevant contact. Hopefully, with a decent black book, we should be able to link directly with the right people.

Frequently, business owners have a wealth of positive connections in their black book that they have not leveraged.

Some talk themselves out of making contact with thoughts like:

'I haven't been in touch for so long that it seems rude now to go back just because I want help.'

'I don't know what to say or how to approach them.'

'I am unclear about what I am doing, so I can't approach them yet.'

'I haven't got time to do it.'

'I am not sure if this contact is relevant anymore.'

These blocks can be overcome by opening your mind to the potential value of your black book and being open to exploring a positive way of approaching them.

Quick Questions

Do you have a black book of contacts?

Why might you need to contact those in your black book?

Quick Win
Review your black book – what does it look like?

At its core, you will have contacts with whom you are close and have a strong and trusting relationship. In the inner circle will be contacts outside your core, with whom you might have had a strong relationship in the past, but have lost touch. In the outer circle will be peripheral contacts who you are not that close to anymore: you may have only met them once, but you connected.

Think about how you can move contacts from your outer to inner circle, or from your inner circle to the core.

How to do it
Here are some steps you may want to consider:

- Send an email first or a message through LinkedIn to reintroduce yourself

- Refer to your shared past and why you are making contact – make it about helping each other, not just about you

- Keep it short and light

- Suggest a call or meet-up

- Follow up and thank them.

Here are some methods you might want to use:

- Use opportunities to meet by sharing something that you are doing or attending that might interest them

- Invite them to play golf or attend a sporting event that interests them

- Look for joint presentation opportunities where you both could add value

- Offer a friendly 'Hi, how are you doing?' catch-up call or coffee

- Send something of interest or relevance to them.

Quick Success

Neil, a finance director working with a number of companies, understood the power of his black book when he started up as an independent finance director. He had a strong corporate background, having been well thought of and successful in all his previous roles.

Initially, he was reluctant to work his black book. He used the excuse of not having enough time, but the reality was that he was unsure how to position himself with his new business, and what he wanted from his contacts.

Once he realised that this was the case, he spent some time thinking through his black book strategy. He knew that many of his contacts enjoyed playing golf, and as a keen player himself, he figured this was the ideal way to work his black book in a relaxed environment.

So, regular invitations to great golf courses and relaxed lunches became the new way forward for Neil's black book. The result has been a series of mutually beneficial conversations and a full order book for Neil. He has also kept himself fit in the process!

Quick Actions

Make a list of your own black book contacts.

Decide on the best approach for each.

Task yourself to make one black book approach each week.

18: Ask for referrals and recommendations

'When you trust a person, you are more likely to trust the business they recommend you.'

There really is no better way to get new business easily than a referral or strong recommendation from someone who is already sold on your product or services.

You will find that business which comes from a referral or recommendation is frequently a virtual guarantee of success. The more trust the potential prospect has in the person that refers or recommends, the more likely they are to buy from you.

You can always get good referrals from satisfied customers, trusted alliances, suppliers and other good network contacts who know the kind of clients you are looking for and who hold you or your services in high esteem.

Many people don't like to ask for referrals or recommendations, although the majority are very happy to receive them. Many will admit to not being as active in encouraging them as they could be.

The reality is that when you have delivered to a standard that delights your customer, most will be more than happy to refer you. Or, similarly, if a business contact knows exactly what you are looking for and trusts in the quality of your service, they too should be happy to refer you on to good opportunities. Most people do like to help, especially when it is acknowledged and appreciated.

The biggest challenge tends to be remembering to ask your clients and contacts for referrals in the first place. Getting those referral contact details might be your priority, but it is not always as important to those you are asking, especially when they are busy. You may find yourself having to do quite a bit of prompting to make it happen.

Quick Questions
How much of your new business during this last year came from referrals or recommendations?

Who is your best referrer?

How many referrals have you given to your contacts?

Quick Win
If you want to increase your number of referrals and recommendations, you will need a strategy. You will also need to think about the best way to request them and to motivate your contacts into action.

Getting the perfect referral
There will be a certain type of referral or recommendation that will be ideal for your business, and which you will want to encourage. When encouraging referrals, you will need to be clear about the type of problems you can solve and the type of potential customers for whom you are looking. This will enable your referrers to easily

identify the person or company who would benefit from your service or product.

Timing is key when you ask
When you are asking for a referral from an existing client, it is usually best to ask for it at the point of successful delivery. This is when your client is at their most enthusiastic about you and about what you have done for them.

At this stage you might say: 'Do you know of anybody else like you, who might benefit from a service/product such as this?'

Plan what you are going to say
You could try something along the lines of: 'I am really glad that you are happy with the work we have done for you. Most of our new clients come from referrals or recommendations. Do you know of any business owners who are looking for the same kind of results as we were able to accomplish for you?'

Explain how to refer people to you
You need to stay in control here. Just saying, 'If you know someone, just get them to call me' leaves it purely to chance that they will. Instead, you could say: 'If you know someone, could you give me a call, and we can discuss the best way to approach them?'

Another alternative is to ask to be put in touch by email, with both parties copied in, along with a link to your website. This leaves it up to both of you to make contact, but it is easy for somebody to set up, doesn't take much time, and you now have each other's email addresses.

Create a perfect referral description

You may also want to ask your referrer to provide some specific information about the business case or person's requirements. This is possible when you are working closely with an alliance or networking contact, or when there is an incentive involved. You can be more prescriptive in this instance.

It may be advisable to spend some time helping your potential referrer to get to know your business and your ideal customers. The more they understand, the more likely they are to see the right opportunities for you.

Motivate referrals with an experience of your service at no cost

If you are starting up or have developed a new product or service, providing a no-cost experience can be a great way of creating a case study and generating referrals from it. If your contact has had a positive experience at no cost, they are more likely to make the effort to refer your services.

Make sure you choose the right contacts for offers such as these. You need to choose someone who has a wide enough network and the right contacts for you.

Motivate referrals with incentives

In some cases, offering a gift or incentive for both the referrer and the referee can create positive momentum. For example, if you receive a free bottle of wine with your next meal for referring a friend to a restaurant, and the friend gets the same offer, you both benefit and you will probably keep going back for more. These incentives can keep running.

Reward and show appreciation for referrals

If you get a good piece of business from a referrer, make sure you show your appreciation. This could be a simple thank you or a gift. The chances of that person doing it again for you when they feel appreciated are much higher.

You could also consider referral incentives to encourage customers and contacts to offer you referrals. Sometimes the feel-good factor which comes from helping you is enough, but a reciprocal referral is always a nice touch.

Quick Success

David, the director of a market intelligence business, had developed a new product called 'Customer Pathfinder'. This product had been created to enable business owners to take the right path when developing, positioning and marketing their business, guided by insightful customer feedback.

David offered me an opportunity to test the product with no charge. We worked together to craft the right questions for the customer interviews and to structure the report in such a way that would make it easy for me to access and use the feedback. We also discussed generating case studies from the process.

The project was a great success – the case studies were invaluable and the customer feedback helped me to make some important decisions for growing my business. The whole process also boosted my own personal confidence in the real practical and emotional value of the mentoring I undertake.

Having had this very positive experience, I subsequently felt very confident in referring David's 'Customer Pathfinder' service to my clients. I constantly see opportunities for the 'Customer Pathfinder' and David and his partner Matt receive many good quality referrals from me.

On the back of this success, they have now developed another product called 'Prospect Pathfinder', focusing on building sales lists and generating appointments, which I am also happy to refer to my clients. I have become one of their best referral partners.

Quick Actions
Ask three existing customers for a referral using the suggestions outlined above.

Put together a description of your perfect referral and discuss it with your contacts and colleagues.

Consider offering an incentive for the perfect referral.

19: Develop an opportunity radar

'Opportunities are everywhere for those who have the eyes to see them.'

Having an 'opportunity radar' is the ability to see or hear opportunities yourself or for others, taking the appropriate actions to explore that opportunity and make something happen. It is about shining the light and seeing what lies hidden in the darkness. An example could be hearing someone express a need or a problem, picking up on it and exploring whether you or one of your contacts could help.

In my experience, some people have a natural opportunity radar, seeing and hearing opportunities everywhere, whereas others seem to be blind to everything in front of them unless it directly affects them.

I have defined some of the characteristics and skills of those who have a natural opportunity radar.

Someone who has it . . .

- Is open and curious

- Hears problems and wants to solve them

- Picks up on things they hear and see

- Is a good networker

- Is focused on others and wants to help

- Always follows up but is not pushy.

Quick Questions

Where are you on the opportunity radar scale? Rate your-self from 1 to 10, 1 being the lowest and 10 the highest.

What is stopping or blocking your radar?

What could you do differently?

Quick Win

Having or developing an opportunity radar is a question of attitude. There is a certain mindset supported by a set of beliefs that, once engaged with, will ensure your radar is switched on.

Take a moment and try to see the world through the filter of the following set of beliefs. They may already be your beliefs – they are certainly mine.

- Helping people is a good thing

- Opportunities are everywhere

- I really believe in the value of what I have/can do for the right people

- People get a lift when you help them or pass an opportunity their way

- The right people/situations come on your path for a reason; you just need to be aware and open when they do

- There is a potential opportunity in every situation – it's just a matter of uncovering it.

You are much more likely to see and attract opportunities to you if you have already defined the opportunities you desire. Once you articulate what it is you want, it is as if you are making a request. You want something to happen, and things do have a habit of finding you when you ask for it clearly enough.

I have had many experiences with mentoring clients who, having completed their ideal target client definition, found that they suddenly received a call or a referral for someone that fitted the bill exactly. It is not always that easy, of course, but it definitely helps to be clear about the opportunities you want to find.

The same principle applies to seeking out opportunities for others. Help them to articulate clearly what it is they need, narrow it down if needs be to something precise, and then when that particular opportunity passes your radar, you will be in a position to help them.

This creates a virtuous circle – people love it when you have listened to their needs and present them with a ready-made solution, making it far more likely that they will return the favour.

Quick Success

Alison runs an accountancy and book-keeping business and is a member of my sales and marketing academy. I ran a session on developing an opportunity radar, as I wanted to help the group see more opportunities for both themselves and for others.

Alison loved the concept and really engaged with it. She realised that the mindset and beliefs I had described were very close to how she naturally thought, but she had not been aware of this before. This consciousness made a big difference to Alison – it was like switching on a light bulb in her head.

Working with Alison over a period of time, I noticed not only how many new client opportunities she seemed to be finding for herself each month, but how many opportunities she was also seeing for others in the group. She always seemed to be suggesting something for someone. She even went out to her local networking group and gave a talk on the subject.

She now has her opportunity radar firmly switched on.

Quick Actions
Define the opportunities that you want.

Switch your opportunity radar on and see what happens.

20: Use special offers and incentives

'Everyone likes a bargain in which they see value.'

A special offer is an opportunity for a customer to gain an advantage that should be perceived as irresistible. A special offer should motivate purchasing decisions.

Special offers can help to achieve any number of desired outcomes, such as introducing customers to new products, speeding up the buying cycle or moving old and unwanted stock. We are all motivated by a good deal: getting something we want at a lower price than we would normally pay.

Quick Question
What special offers or incentives have motivated you to buy in the past?

Quick Win
When creating your special offer, you need to understand the psychology of the 'Risk–Reward' thought process that takes place in the mind of your prospective customer.

Whenever somebody considers buying anything, they will weigh up the benefits or values they will receive versus their level of risk; i.e. how much they have to give or pay in return. If the perceived value is low but the perceived risk is high, the chances are that the person will be reluctant to buy. If the perceived risk is low and the value is high, then there is every chance a sale will be made.

So the best, most irresistible special offers are the ones that increase the perceived value whilst lowering the perceived risk.

How to increase perceived value

- Offer two for the price of one, or a multi-buy discount – supermarkets do this well

- Package complimentary products together with a lower overall price compared to buying the products separately – spas and beauty salons are good at this

- Discount the price as an introductory offer for a limited period of time

- Add in extra bonuses – 'How To' e-book sellers are very adept at this.

How to decrease the perceived risk

- Provide low, affordable payment terms – car retailers frequently offer this facility

- Interest-free credit – furniture and electrical retailers utilise this prominently

- Delay payments with no accrued interest – buy now, pay later

- Give free thirty-day trial periods

- Give access to follow-up support help after the sale has been made – computer software companies market this add-on

- Give proof of the results of the product or service using real-life case studies

- Endorse the product or service with testimonials.

If you combine a technique which increases perceived value with one that decreases perceived risk, you will enjoy an increased response rate to your special offer or incentive.

Integrate special offers and incentives into your sales and marketing strategy. Try various offers and test them out in your advertising, email marketing, networking and any other marketing communication you engage in with new potential customers.

Find the combination that works best for you.

Quick Success

I am a member of B4, which is a leading business-to-business network in the Thames Valley, helping to promote local businesses of all shapes and sizes. They run networking events and publish magazines for the benefit of their members, as well as operating a free listings guide, *Living in Oxford*, and a unique online discount website, Vouch. *Living in Oxford*, B4 and Vouch are part of the In Oxford Group (IOG).

The IOG have always been innovative when it comes to special offers, and in leveraging on their business contacts and capabilities accordingly.

One recent example is their involvement with 'Flowers @ Oxford', an annual event held every August at Lady Margaret Hall, Oxford University, 'for a celebration of all things floral'.

The IOG helps to review and publicise the event via its various listings, and also offers discounted accommodation for those visiting the event. Anybody looking to book accommodation for 'Flowers @ Oxford' via the official website is directed to IOG, who offer a range of hotels with the best available rates.

Additionally, the special offer includes a complimentary food voucher for an Oxford restaurant (via the Vouch website), plus complimentary copies of their magazines, including *Living in Oxford*, *The Oxford Map* and *The Oxfordshire Restaurant Guide*.

In this manner, IOG manages to leverage all of its contacts and deliver value for them via increased publicity and business traffic, whilst offering superb value for money to the 'Flowers @ Oxford' visitors – a true win-win scenario.

Quick Actions

Come up with an irresistible special offer to attract new customers.

Decide how you will increase perceived value and decrease perceived risk.

Measure its success.

Chapter Review

Quick Wins to Attract Top-Quality Leads

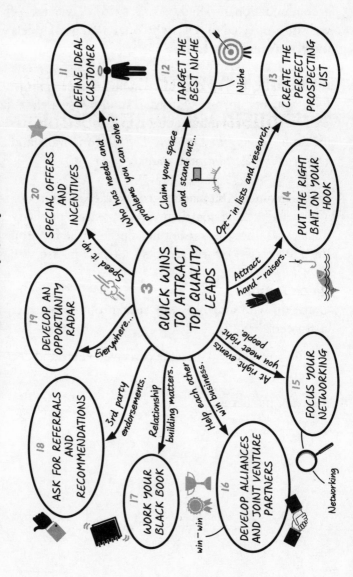

3 QUICK WINS TO ATTRACT TOP QUALITY LEADS

11 DEFINE IDEAL CUSTOMER

12 TARGET THE BEST NICHE — Niche

13 CREATE THE PERFECT PROSPECTING LIST

14 PUT THE RIGHT BAIT ON YOUR HOOK

15 FOCUS YOUR NETWORKING — Networking

16 DEVELOP ALLIANCES AND JOINT VENTURE PARTNERS — win – win

17 WORK YOUR BLACK BOOK

18 ASK FOR REFERRALS AND RECOMMENDATIONS

19 DEVELOP AN OPPORTUNITY RADAR

20 SPECIAL OFFERS AND INCENTIVES

Who has needs and problems you can solve?

Claim your space and stand out...

Opt – in lists and research.

Attract hand – raisers.

At right events you meet right people.

Help each other win business.

Relationship building matters.

3rd party endorsements.

Everywhere...

Speed it up?

CHAPTER 4:
Quick Wins to Build Strong Business Relationships

21: Trust your instincts

'Listen to your instincts – they are trying to tell you something important.'

Instincts can be described as a gut reaction or inner feeling that goes beyond logic or facts. Sometimes you can feel that something is not quite right but are unable to explain it logically. Or you may have a sense that something or someone is right, but can't back it up with facts and figures.

Your instincts are like an inner voice that comes from deep within and that seems to know what the best course of action is. Think of it as your instincts trying to protect you.

Everyone will have experienced the feeling of being about to undertake a certain course of action, then hearing an inner voice telling them not to do it. Likewise, you will probably have had the feeling of something being just right, moved heaven and earth to make it happen, and been proved spot-on with the risk you took. However, we tend to dwell on our failures, not our successes, hence the well-known phrase: 'I should have trusted my instincts.'

Our inner wisdom often knows more than we give it credit for, so if you don't pay attention to it, you may miss important information. Your instinct can be drowned out by too much noise or other distractions, and equally it can be brought alive by peace and space.

I notice the difference when I give myself that space and time, at the beginning or end of a busy day, to connect with my instinct. For me it can be a morning run, a bike ride, an evening meditation or a quiet walk by the river. When I relax, my inner voice usually comes to me and sheds light on whatever it is that needs clarifying.

Quick Questions
When was the last time your instinct gave you a strong message?

What was the result?

Quick Win
Accessing the power of your instinct is all about trust. You need to give yourself space, turn down the volume of your inner chatter, and allow your own wisdom to be heard.

The more able you are to free your mind from the constant 'busyness' which keeps it occupied, the more likely you are to hear your inner voice inside that might have something important you need to hear.

Your instinct is a feeling, a knowing; something in the pit of your stomach that tells you something is right or not right. Give yourself time to feel. Don't make yourself so busy that you lose all sensation.

Take time out to connect with nature. Go for a walk, a run, a cycle ride. Or simply sit somewhere quiet and enjoy the silence. Take some deep breaths and let go of all the stress of the day. Enjoy just being and doing nothing, even if it is only for half an hour. You will be surprised at the positive effect something this simple can have on your ability to connect properly with your instincts.

We are not machines and we can't just keep running and running without care and attention. Your soul needs nurturing as much as your customers need serving.

Take care of your instinct, and it will reward you with its wisdom.

Quick Success

I have had a number of experiences in my life when I have ignored my instincts, only to find that the warnings they gave me came true in the end. I remember being about to embark on a business relationship with a partner, to work on a project for which I had a lot of passion. I heard a voice at the time saying this was the wrong move for me, but I ignored it because on paper there were a number of very positive things in the relationship's favour.

Sadly, the project didn't take off, but I wasn't entirely surprised as I never really felt that my partner and I had the right relationship. If I had listened to my instincts, I would have avoided a lot of wasted time and effort going down a road that wasn't right for me. I learnt a lot from that mistake.

One year after that experience, I was offered help in my business from the partner of one of my trusted colleagues. However, at our first meeting I wasn't sure that I connected with him that much, despite the fact he was a very intelligent and experienced businessman. I was quite negative and defensive at the time, as I was still sore from the previous business relationship that had gone wrong. I wasn't sure I wanted any help. I remember going home that evening, standing on my courtyard and looking up at the neighbouring church spire, asking myself what I should do. My instinct said 'See him again, but be open about your concerns'.

I tried to argue with myself but my instinct won through. On the second meeting I got to know him better and I saw things that I had missed the first time round. I ended up taking up his offer of some business advice and mentoring and now he is one of my partners in Heart of Business. He is very different from me in many ways, but we complement each other's strengths and he has been great to work with. That is one experience where I could easily have walked away, but am glad that I listened to my instinct.

Quick Actions
Make a decision to listen to your instinct for a week.

Give yourself a bit of space and time to access it.

Write down some of the messages you get.

22: Share your values

*'When you use your values as your guiding light,
you can see more clearly.'*

Your values are what really matter to you, in your life and your business. They can ignite your passion and fuel your frustration. Values can be described using words and phrases such as trust, integrity, honesty, quality standards, putting the customer first, team engagement, clear communication, creativity, having fun and caring relationships.

It is important to describe what our values mean to us, and how we define them, as one person's definition of a particular value may be completely different from another's. For example, to one person, trust may mean showing that a person's opinion is valued by listening and following through on agreed actions, whereas to another it may mean being consistent and respectful in communication style and behaviour.

Values are at the core of all human relationships. We all tend to like people who behave in a way that we engage and connect with. Rapport is greater with those we understand and who understand us.

Sharing values doesn't mean that you have to share the same strengths and skill sets. You can be very different people but knowing that you agree at the core makes it easier to appreciate and respect the contribution each person has to make.

Frustration in business relationships often stems from not agreeing with other people's behaviours or methods of communication. We feel that they are not doing what we believe they should be doing or vice versa. In this sense, they have in some way violated what is important to us.

This could be the client who continually changes things at the last minute, the colleague who never follows through on his commitments, the supplier who doesn't communicate with you during a project, or the team member who always arrives late.

You may also notice the opposite when the people you work with behave in a way that makes you feel good. They always get back to you when they say they will, they are always prepared for meetings, they turn up on time, they are respectful in their communication, and they take the actions to which they have committed.

The key to understanding values and the behaviours they represent is awareness. If you know what values are important to you, what 'good and bad look like' in terms of that value in action, it is easier to recognise and communicate them to others.

If you choose people to work with who you know share similar values, you are far more likely to enjoy a harmonious business relationship.

Once you are clear about your personal and business values, you can use those values as a filter to make decisions and choices. Those decisions might be about the suppliers you choose to work with, the people in your team, or the clients you choose to deal with.

Quick Questions
What really matters to you in terms of your relationships with people in business – what do you value highly?

What would each of these values look like in action?

Quick Win
The most important thing is to begin by clarifying your own business values. Make a list of what is most important to you in your business and use words that mean something to you and your team.

For each of those values, try and describe what they mean. (In the 'Quick Success' section below, there is an example of this exercise for my business, which is values-driven.)

Once you have described those values, you can begin to consider how you are delivering them in terms of both your approach to customers and your interaction with your team.

Can you identify where you are strong or weak? Are you truly living your values or could you improve?

At a more personal level, you can explore what really matters to any individual by asking questions and really listening carefully to what they say to you. People will always place an emphasis on their values.

Good questions to ask to uncover values:

What is really important to you? – What would I need to do more of to give you that?

What matters most to you? – What shows you that you are getting the things that matter?

What frustrates you? – What would put this right?

Quick Success

Heart of Business is a brand that is driven by a core set of values. These values are the guiding light that helps us (myself and my partners) choose the people that we want to be part of our business. They also guide how we work together as a team, and how we work with our customers.

If we go off-track, we always come back to these values and ask ourselves what behaviour would mean that we were being true to our values. It has helped us to overcome challenges growing this business.

This is our description of these values and what they mean:

Heart of Business is based on a foundation of solid core values, which support our aim to inspire and deliver mutually beneficial results for all our stakeholders, namely:

Our customers and clients

Our employees and members

Our suppliers and partners

Our investors

The communities in which we operate.

We aim to conduct our business by adhering to our core values, which are as follows:

Integrity and trust
Reason: Knowing you have trust in your relationships gives you strength.

Integrity and trust are at the foundation of all our relationships with others. We encourage sincerity, openness in approach, and authentic, honest communication.

Challenge constructively
Reason: Knowing that you are safe to try new ways of thinking and acting gives you courage.
Constructive challenge ensures that everyone gives of their best and collectively delivers exceptional service and value. We encourage boundaries to be stretched in order to achieve MORE.

Pride and passion
Reason: Having passion and a sense of pride in the business you are part of gives you great motivation.
Our pride and passion for Heart of Business and what it represents is the seed from which strong roots can grow. These roots form the basis of a business with which others will be proud to be associated.

Quality standards
Reason: Having quality standards ensures that your best is recognised.

Striving to deliver consistent standards of excellence ensures that we all deliver real value. We encourage clarity and focus in order to reach and maintain the standards we set.

Love
Reason: Having love at the centre of what you do makes everything worthwhile.
Love is at the core of our approach. We care about your success – we want the best for you, and for you to be your best.

Team engagement
Reason: Understanding and appreciating the expertise in others means that together we are stronger.
We ensure that everyone working to serve our customers are fully committed and respected for the valuable role they perform.

Freshness/innovation
Reason: Keeping things current means that you stay ahead.
We embrace change and aim to keep ourselves at the forefront of innovation, so that we can consistently inspire our clients and team members with creative ideas and fresh outlooks.

Focused action
Reason: Important results are only achieved if action is taken.
We encourage action and will guide our customers on the steps they need to take to move their business forward.

Quick Actions

Take time to consider your own business values.

Work with the team to describe your values in action.

Use them in your marketing communications and sales presentations.

Set your values as your filter for decisions and actions.

23: Listen mindfully

'Being truly heard is every person's joy.'

To be listened to is important to all of us – it is a sign of respect and interest.

True listening only occurs when there is a total focus on the speaker. When you truly listen, you understand what the speaker both says and feels. In your mind's eye, you are able to walk a mile in their shoes. Listening is magic when undertaken mindfully.

You may think you are listening, but are you really? So many things get in the way of truly hearing what another person has to say.

Most of us approach our interactions with a head full of our own thoughts, feelings and experiences, our minds preoccupied with our own beliefs, values and assumptions. With all this background noise going on, it can be almost impossible to clearly hear the voice of another.

Allowing yourself to become distracted, or being overly keen to move the conversation on to where you want it to be, will both get in the way of listening mindfully.

Ask yourself, do you ever:

- Become distracted whilst listening

- Interrupt with one of your own opinions, ideas or stories before the person has finished

- Try to move the conversation on to what you want to talk about

- Misinterpret or misunderstand what has just been said

- Ask irrelevant questions

- Talk too much

- Disagree, or get upset and defensive very quickly.

Listening is a conscious decision. To do it well, you need to place your own perceptions to one side, and give the speaker your full attention.

Those who are skilled listeners are able hear more than just the words. They will hear the speaker's:

- concerns and desires
- opinions and perceptions
- beliefs and values
- feelings and emotions
- needs.

They will also be aware of non-verbal communication: body language, voice tone and conversational pace. Good listeners are able to get to the core of what matters most to the person to whom they are listening.

Mindfully listening to your potential clients will enable you to find out not only their needs, but also their values, and who they are as people. When they feel heard, it will build rapport and increase the likelihood of them doing business with you.

When you listen mindfully to your team members, you will help them to feel valued, increasing motivation and loyalty in the process.

Quick Questions

Can you remember the last time you were really listened to?

How did it feel to have someone's complete focus and attention, and to know that listening to you was really important to them?

Quick Win

Listening can be a selfless activity. It is more about the other person than it is about you. You will need to relax, and be in the right mental and emotional state to be able to give the speaker your full attention – this is the first step to good listening

Get yourself into a listening state by preparing yourself beforehand. If you have been busy and have a lot on your mind, give yourself ten minutes to clear your head first and relax.

Arrange a place to meet that is quiet, calm and free from distractions. Seating works better at a round table, or at right angles, be it in a lounge or a meeting room. To listen fully you need to stay in the moment, suspend any judgements and be patient.

Wait – adopt a beginners' mindset, and be curious about what the speaker has to say. Be comfortable with any silences.

Make sure that you look at your speaker, ask relevant questions, and summarize from time to time to confirm your understanding of their issues. If you need clarification, ask for it, and paraphrase what you are hearing to make sure you have got it right.

Notice your speaker's responses, pick up on their language and, where appropriate, feed it back to them. This will make the person feel heard.

Notice the energy, tone and pace of the speaker's voice. Match that energy and pace when you ask questions and summarize. This will help you to maintain rapport and, again, make your speaker feel heard.

Give out positive body language cues that you are interested: nodding, open hands, eye contact, smiling as appropriate, relaxed breathing, or leaning forward. Avoid frowning, glaring, slumping, sighing – the non-verbal signs of negative thoughts about what the speaker is saying.

Make sure that you are able to communicate to them exactly what their priorities are, and what matters most, in any follow-up action or proposal. This is important, as follow-through is vital to maintaining the trust built from mindful listening.

Quick Success

I am a supporter of my Global Retreat Centre near Oxford, which is run by the Brahma Kumaris World Spiritual University. I have attended a number of their lectures, meditation courses, retreat days and the wonderful 'Peace in the Park' event that they run each year.

On one particular retreat day, I attended a seminar discussion on 'Listening Mindfully'. During this discussion, we were asked to undertake a very simple exercise to demonstrate what it is like to listen for five minutes to someone without interrupting or interjecting, and that person to be the sole focus of our attention for those five minutes.

The subject we had to talk about was what we were proud of in our lives. After giving the person five minutes to talk, the listener had to reflect back what they had heard about what was important to the person they had been listening to. There was no note-taking, just complete engagement with the other person for a full five minutes.

The exercise was amazing. Afterwards, everybody realised how good it felt simply to be heard, and also how tempting it can be to butt in or ask questions. For some people it was quite an emotional experience as they were talking about very personal matters.

Giving people the space just to talk, whilst not trying to fill in the silences, is a very powerful and positive technique. The feeling of being heard is one of the great gifts you can give another person.

Quick Actions

If, having read this section, you recognise that your own listening skills require improvement, start by becoming aware of what happens to you when you are listening to other people.

Take notice of your physical and emotional reactions, and your own listening or non-listening behaviours.

Make a conscious decision to listen more mindfully, and then notice what impact this has on your relationships with clients and colleagues.

24: Keep in touch

'If you care enough, you keep in touch.'

In order to keep any relationship alive, you need to keep in touch. We all have so many different business relationships and if you don't physically see or talk to someone regularly it can be easy to lose the connection.

You may meet some potential alliance partners who could be great to work with, but if you see them once and then don't keep in touch in some way, you disappear from each other's radar. This means that when an opportunity comes up to work together, you will probably be forgotten.

It is the same with any potential networking contacts you meet – there may not have been a need to do business at the time, but five years later a need may arise, and if you have not been keeping in touch it is unlikely that you will be contacted.

There are so many different ways you can keep in touch with your colleagues, alliances, customers and friends these days that it should be relatively easy to keep those channels of communication open. All you need to do is to put a system in place and then work that system.

To keep in touch you can use:

- Social media – Facebook and LinkedIn

- A regular customer bulletin or newsletter

- Free tips and information that could be valuable

- A friendly email

- An occasional call

- A referral

- A coffee, lunch or invite to a special event.

Keeping in touch, however you go about it, reminds your contacts that you care about their interests and needs.

Quick Question
What systems do you have in place to keep in touch with your important contacts?

Quick Win
It does take time and focus to keep in touch with people and to do it with care. It is time well spent if the relationships are worth keeping in touch with.

The starting point is to have a plan and then create some systems around that to enable you and your team to implement a number of 'touches' that both maintain and build your relationships.

Your plan may include a communication calendar. A communication calendar is your plan for all the individual touches you plan to make over the course of any twelve-month period. It is a complete schedule of events and activities. It could be through email, social media, blogs, newsletters, information updates, telephone calls, social events, free talks, direct mail promotions or website links. You need to have a calendar that offers exactly the right amount of touches. Your customers will not want to be bombarded with information.

Each part of your plan should ultimately fit together like the pieces of a jigsaw puzzle. Each element can support and link to each other.

Your newsletter or bulletin can be used to deliver useful information as well as promote an aspect of your business that your customer will find of value. The promotion that you choose can then be linked to your website and links provided in the newsletter to encourage traffic.

The telephone calls you make to update customer records can be linked to invitations to events or customer needs reviews.

Direct mail and email updates can be run concurrently, enabling one to support the other.

Creating a newsletter

A newsletter is something that you produce and distribute to your customers, usually once a month. Newsletters can be distributed electronically using a system like MailChimp or in a traditional hard copy format by post. Newsletters are one of the most powerful tools for keeping your name uppermost with your contacts, customers and colleagues. It is an easy way to reach a large number of people. I have been sending out my sales and marketing newsletter for a number of years – some people had been on my mailing list for up to five years before becoming customers, but having received my tips and ideas regularly, they all felt that they knew me and had a relationship with me – that is the power of a regular newsletter.

What makes a newsletter work?
A name
This will give it an identity and brand of its own and will become memorable to the receivers. The name needs to convey value to the receiver.

Useful content
Content can be made up of news, answers to questions, ideas, tips, case studies, articles, recommendations, updates and anything that has perceived value which your customers will look forward to receiving.

The right length
Most people will tell you that they suffer from information overload, so consider how you can make your newsletter both interesting and easy to read. Headlines with snappy titles and 'Read More' links are more powerful than reams of copy. People will read what they are interested in, so make your newsletter relevant to your audience.

Social Media
A well-planned and delivered social media strategy has numerous touch points, but it can be time-consuming and you do need to know what you are doing for it to work well. I would advise focusing on the social media channel that is most likely to be viewed by your target audience.

LinkedIn is a great way to keep in touch with your business to business contacts, whilst Facebook and Twitter tend to demand daily attention and work better for consumer-led products or services.

If you are going to do this yourself, do get some expert training so that you know how to set your profiles up correctly and can use the vast array of free tools available. The other option is to outsource your social media delivery to an expert who manages and delivers it for you, or to recruit a marketing assistant. For many busy business owners this may be the preferred option. Having someone in your business who is focused on maintaining and delivering your communication calendar is important.

Quick Success

By keeping in touch, I won a new mentoring client who I had first met five years ago at a training course. At the time we swapped business cards, and I asked her if she would like to receive my monthly newsletter. She said yes, so I entered her into my newsletter database and connected with her on LinkedIn.

At the time her business was very small and she operated from home. Five years later, her business had expanded significantly, with an office in London and a healthy turnover of nearly half a million pounds. At that stage, she gave me a call as she was looking for a business mentor to help her and her team to move to the next stage.

I got the call because I had stayed in touch and kept the connection. She felt she still knew me, and what I had to offer.

I have many examples like this, where keeping in touch has retained enough of a connection, be it for a business owner I may have met at an event, at a talk I delivered, or whilst networking some years back. By remaining 'present', they consider me when they do need some help to grow their business. I encourage my mentoring clients to create a 'keep in touch' strategy, and those that do find that it pays dividends in the long term.

Quick Actions

Create a communication calendar.

Come up with ideas for a newsletter or expert tips bulletin.

Explore outsourcing your social media.

25: Address problems positively

'Try to see an opportunity in every difficulty – there is always one there.'

Every business, from time to time, will experience customer dissatisfaction. Nobody is perfect. Mistakes happen. It is how you deal with them that will make the biggest difference to your relationships.

It can be easy to drive customers away if their complaints or problems are badly handled or ignored. A complaint is a statement about expectations that have not been met, but it can be a gift, if you choose to see it that way. Your clients and customers have two options when they feel dissatisfied: they can either talk to you or walk away. If they just walk away, then you have no opportunity to solve the problem – you may not even know what it is.

Many people fail to complain even though they are unhappy because they don't want to bother anyone, because they prefer to avoid confrontation, or because they simply don't know how to complain. However, they will probably express their dissatisfaction to others – anecdotal evidence suggests that one in five people tell up to twenty others when they are unhappy. Hence, one complaint can very quickly turn into negative marketing, something of which large corporates are acutely aware.

If you are told about a problem, or if a customer has the courage to complain, look upon it positively. It gives you the opportunity to learn more about your business, to solve the problem, to retain the customer, and to ensure that the feedback about you afterwards is positive.

Customer relationships are frequently enhanced as the result of a well-handled problem. Show your customers how much you care about them, by giving them the service they deserve.

Quick Questions
What problems in your business have led to customer dissatisfaction?

How did you deal with it?

Quick Win
You need to create an atmosphere within your business that encourages customers to complain if they feel that their expectations have not been met.

You will need a system for handling complaints that can immediately provide the required 'feel-good' factor. You and your team need to listen, and put your values into practice by delivering exactly what you promise.

How to deal positively with problems and complaints

- Listen, understand what the customer is dissatisfied about, and apologise

- Offer a solution that gives the customer more than they expect – put a smile on their face

- Learn from it and put systems in place to minimise the chances of the same mistake happening again

- Allow the customer to express any negative emotions connected with the complaint without taking it personally. Remember they are complaining about the product or service, not about you personally

- Ask questions to clarify your understanding of the problem and take notes, the more visibly the better. When the customer feels heard, you will be able to express your appreciation of their feelings and apologise.

Here are some phrases that will help ensure that the customer feels that his or her frustrations are understood:

'I appreciate that this must have been very frustrating for you. We apologise for the inconvenience that it has caused you. We would like the opportunity to put this right for you immediately.'

'Thank you for bringing this to our attention. It must have been frustrating to have this happen. Please accept our sincere apologies. Can I suggest some possible solutions – which solution would best suit you?'

Give your customer a choice of solutions. This will give him or her a feeling of control, which is frequently what the customer feels has been lost when something goes wrong.

Make sure you and your team keep a complaints log. This complaints log should include the date, customer details, complaint details, cause, solution provided and, most importantly, system changes to ensure the complaint does not reoccur.

Quick Success

We use a local hotel by the River Thames for our Heart of Business team events. As part of these events we have a sit-down buffet lunch. Along with our existing members, we invite a selection of guests who want to experience the Heart of Business concept before joining. Everyone pays an event fee to come along.

The hotel's event manager was very conscientious, and before our first event spent time understanding our needs and the importance of creating a positive customer experience – especially as ours was a growing business and could potentially become a regular booking.

The first lunch we had was not quite up to standard and I gave feedback to the event manager and the chef. As a result, the lunch and the presentation subsequently improved significantly, and the feedback from everyone was excellent. I also passed that positive feedback on to the hotel manager, reinforcing the difference it made to us when the lunch was good.

Unfortunately, on the fourth meeting the standard had dropped again, resulting in a few members complaining that they had enjoyed the meeting but not the lunch. I went back to the event manager and had a meeting with the chef. They listened, took the feedback and apologised. They asked us again what we wanted and reflected this back in an excellent menu choice and reassurance that this would be delivered to the standard we required in order to make the event a positive experience for our members.

Consequently, the food and the service in the restaurant have improved, the location is wonderful and the event manager is always checking that we are happy with everything. The lines of communication remain open for future feedback, but recent experience has shown that when feedback is given constructively and honestly, things do change for the better.

Quick Actions

Write down what you learnt the last time one of your customers complained.

Set up a feedback system.

Ensure you regularly get feedback from your customers so that you deal with any problems before they turn into complaints.

Chapter Review

Quick Wins to Build Strong Business Relationships

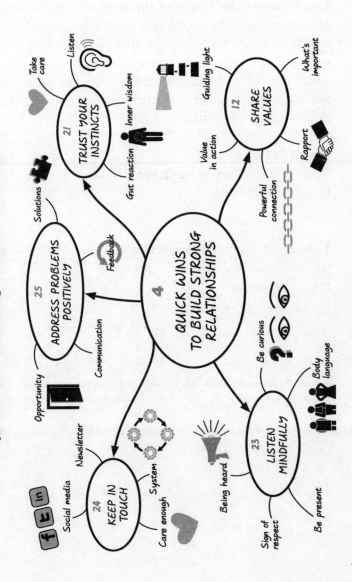

CHAPTER 5:
Quick Wins to Make Your Marketing Work

26. Create a strong brand image
27. Clarify your offering
28. Know your USP
29. Position your expertise
30. Get your key messages right
31. Choose the right marketing methods to get leads
32. Write a simple marketing plan
33. Brief suppliers effectively
34. Promote Success
35. Test and measure ROI

26: Create a strong brand image

'Your business brand is your statement to your market.'

A brand image is far from being just a snazzy name and a nice bit of artwork. Many people think that a brand is simply a company's logo or corporate identity. It is much more than that. Your brand is the face of your business. It is the memorable message that is created when a company promotes the emotional connection it wants its customers to have with its business, its service or its product.

It is not just national and international businesses that require a brand image. Whatever size of business you are, you need to have a clear identity and be memorable in your marketplace. The stronger your brand image, the more likely you are to sustain business growth and customer support.

Many businesses have outgrown their image, or have an image that sends out the wrong messages. I have seen many business images thrown together without any attention to the message behind them, names being chosen because of the business owner's personal history, favourite colours adopted (not necessarily those that work) and images and straplines used that do not make it easy for the customer to connect with what they might be buying.

If you are a new business, you may not have given your brand image any consideration. Your brand identity and strapline needs to reflect the essence of your business, and to communicate this instantly with your market.

Quick Questions

What image are you communicating with your brand?

Is it the image and message you want to create?

Quick Win

Clarity and simplicity are important. You need to be sure what you want to communicate through your image and your core messages. To get this right, you will need to focus on your target market – the people you want to respond to your brand.

How to create your brand image

Step 1: Research

Look at other brands in your market place – what do you like? What works?

Consider what your current brand communicates to your customers.

Ask your customers what they think – get feedback.

Ask the people who don't use your service what they think.

Listen and take notes.

Step 2: Define desired brand values

Create a list of words that describe what customers may want from the service or product you are selling.

For example, from an IT company people may require things such as 'efficiency', 'making the complex simple', 'support' and 'clear, up-to-date advice'.

Brainstorm with your team the words that describe what your customers get from the service or product you deliver.

Again, for an IT company, the phrases you come up with may be 'time- and effort-saving', 'effective working', 'systems that work' and 'advice and support'.

Choose three or four words that describe the 'values' you want your brand to represent.

Taking the IT company again, it might be 'Clarity – Connected – Supported – Efficient'.

Step 3: See the visual impact you want to create
Write down words that describe the image you would like to portray to the marketplace.

The IT company example may use words like 'Simple – Clean – Uncluttered – Minimal'.

Find samples of the visual representations of those messages – look at the images other businesses portray. Decide what you like and collect examples to show your designer.

Notice the impact of colour – choose colours that hit the right emotional buttons for your audience.

Find a designer who listens to exactly what you want to achieve with your brand. Provide a full brief.

Step 4: Fine-tune with feedback
Once some sample images have been created, ask for feedback from a selection of customers, and members of your team. Make sure you ask a broad selection for a balanced view.

Step 5: Create brand guidelines

Once you have made your decision, use your brand image on all your marketing and communications. Consistency is vital.

You need to make sure you get clear brand guidelines created by your designer and then ensure that they are adhered to by everyone in your organisation.

What to do once you have your brand image

Once you have created your brand, you will need to make sure that your market becomes familiar with it. The more familiar your brand becomes, the more trust will be built into it.

Brands become memorable and trusted the more they are seen and heard about in the marketplace, so a brand-building campaign is important. Your brand-building campaign will need to be designed to suit the audience you want to influence and the messages you want associated with your brand.

Ways to create brand awareness:

- A social media campaign
- A PR campaign
- Talks, events and conferences
- Sponsoring floral displays on roundabouts
- Bus and transport advertising
- Banners and signs
- Advertising in publications that reach your market
- Sponsorship of events that reach your market.

To make an impact, your brand needs to be continually in front of your potential customers. You will need to be careful with your advertising budget and choose brand-building methods that will give you both a powerful presence and build trust in your core messages.

Quick Success

A local garage in my home town, Wallingford, was planning to relocate out of a side street and on to a business park. They wanted to change the focus of the company, attract more car servicing business and open a retail store selling motor accessories. This is a family business that had been trading quite happily with the same brand image for over forty years.

Some of the directors of the business were wary of change but Mark, the younger director, saw an opportunity to update their image along with the change of location. Being marketing savvy, he knew that creating a more powerful image locally would have a positive effect on the business.

I was mentoring Mark at the time and we discussed the brand values that were important to communicate to their target market and to the business. I encouraged Mark to do some market research, get feedback from their loyal customer base and explore the local competition. We discussed the feedback with the senior team and worked together to decide on the brand values that were important to communicate through the new image. The values they chose were: 'Care, Service, Fresh, Modern, Great Value and Friendliness'. It was therefore important to communicate these through the new brand.

A designer was briefed fully and an initial set of brand designs created. The senior team chose the design that appealed most after consulting a selection of their customers. They then had the job of ensuring that the new brand was consistently communicated throughout the business. They had newly branded signage both inside and out, a website, flyers, posters, adverts, van livery and more. Every detail was important.

The new image and new location has, as Mark predicted, had a very positive effect on their bottom line. They are flying! I always have my car serviced there and they really are true to their values, do a great job and really care about their customers.

Quick Actions

Review your current brand image.

Decide if it needs a refresh.

Create your own brand brief.

27: Clarify your offering

*'The more clarity there is in your business,
the more able you will be to get results.'*

It is vital to be clear about what you are offering and the value you will be providing. The effectiveness of your communication with customers will be influenced by your own level of clarity.

> **You will need to be clear about:**
>
> • What your proposition is
>
> • How it is structured or packaged
>
> • The value you offer
>
> • The delivery mechanism
>
> • The pricing structure.

It is much easier to sell your products and services when you are clear about what they are and how they interlink. Have you ever not bought from somebody because their message was too confusing, they offered too much, or because the choice simply overwhelmed you? Sometimes less is more.

There is a huge marketplace out there and a tremendous amount of choice. So, buying from someone whose offer has complete clarity, and who can put that information across in a straightforward manner can be an absolute godsend.

Be careful of expanding or tailoring your services to suit every customer request you receive. You risk your proposition broadening to such an extent that it will not be clear whom you serve.

Of course, having the flexibility to adapt and package your services to your customers' precise requirements will add considerable value to your offering, but you must limit yourself to how much you expand your portfolio of services.

Quick Questions

Can you describe your offering clearly and the value it delivers?

Are your customers clear about how they should engage with you?

Quick Win

To gain the clarity you are looking for, you need to take time to do some quality thinking – it may be useful to find someone who can help facilitate this for you.

In order to make sure that your proposition is always geared towards the customers you want to attract, you should:

- Undertake research – market, customer, and competition – to fully understand who you are serving and where your gaps are.

- Listen to feedback from your customers – note down what they repeatedly ask for, or have problems with.

- Critically examine your products and services – how can they provide solutions to these problems?

- Consider creating a visual step-by-step guide or diagram that describes what you offer.

- Think about the different stages of your service – how are they delivered, and what resource is required to do so?

- Consider your prices – how do they compare to your competitors? Are you charging too much or too little?˜

- Test out various product/service packages and pricing with your customers.

- Review your offering from time to time. Focus upon continually improvements so that it remains appealing to your customers.

Once you are clear about your offering, you are in a position to create your unique selling proposition (USP), which you can read about in the next chapter.

Quick Success

Tim and Jayne ran a consultancy and training business, specialising in businesses in the Animal Health sector. They were looking to rebrand and reposition their business, but after our first mentoring session together they realised that they first needed to clarify their offering, which sounded complex and was hard to follow.

Both Tim and Jayne possessed a wealth of experience in their specialist field, which focused upon improving customer experience, using a combination of surveys, training and coaching.

Together, we worked out the core elements of their offering, and structured them into a simple six-stage process with visual aids – this made it much easier for them to explain and for others to follow.

They saw how vital it was to gain this clarity before embarking on spending time, money and effort on marketing materials.

Quick Actions

Take a look at your own offering – how clear is it?

Create a visual step-by-step aid that describes the elements of your service and how they link together.

Obtain customer feedback and adjust accordingly.

28: Know your USP

'Your USP is that extra-special something that makes your service unique.'

Your unique selling proposition – 'USP' – distinguishes you from your competitors and motivates customers to choose your products or services over anybody else's.

It should not be confused with an advertising slogan – it is a statement of 'why' your business is unique.

Some examples of some well-known, successful USPs:

Domino's Pizza – 'Fresh hot pizza in 30 minutes or less, or it's free'

Federal Express – 'When it absolutely, positively has to be there overnight'

AA – 'To our members, we're the fourth emergency service'

Prêt a Manger – 'Chefs at work'.

Many businesses say the same thing, such as 'great customer service', 'quality products' or 'professional service' – these are all admirable qualities, but they don't stand out in marketing messages.

Your challenge is to identify and communicate your uniqueness. You need to be able to talk about something that you do for your customers which is special. You must determine what your customers are not getting from anyone else or what will solve their principal fears or frustrations – then offer it to them!

Quick Questions
What is it that you do that other, similar businesses don't do?

Can you articulate your uniqueness?

Quick Win
Here is how to determine your USP:

- Make a list of what is special and unique about your product or service. Test these on your customers. Do they care?

- Read your testimonials – what positive feedback have you had from your customers? Highlight words and phrases.

- Check out your competitors' advertising. Note down the promises they are making.

- Note down what you could offer that is different from your competition.

- Pick out one or two things about your business which you could make specific and measurable, such as the speed at which you deliver; the quality you produce; the results you are sure you can deliver. Make sure any quality passes the SMART test (Specific, Measurable, Achievable, Relevant and Time-bound).

- Test these USPs in your sales and marketing activities and monitor the responses.

Having carefully crafted your USP, you now need to integrate it into everything that you do.

Quick Success

Here are a couple of examples of companies who went through this process, and clarified their USPs.

Website design company

Problem: Website design companies often confuse their clients with overly technical or jargon-heavy language. They don't always understand how difficult it can be for busy business owners to manage website projects with designers and provide everything in the right order or format. The whole process can be extremely stressful unless it is managed effectively.

What customers want: A marketing focus as opposed to a technical one. Being looked after and guided through a project.

USP 1: A website company with a project manager for every build.

USP 2: A website company that creates a simple marketing machine for your business.

Building company

Problem: Building companies can be slow to produce quotes, and many customers fear that quoted prices can spiral out of control once the job has started. There always seems to be something extra that pops up, and/or jobs that take far longer than estimated.

What customers want: Certainty that the quote will arrive promptly after the initial visit, that there will be some security in the price quoted, and that there will be an estimated time to complete the job.

USP 1: Only seven days from visit to detailed quote.

USP 2: Transparent quotes – if there's any confusion, we'll rectify it.

USP 3: We will fulfil our completion deadlines – if there are any external factors that may affect the deadline, we will notify you right away.

Once you have created an engaging USP, customers will respond positively, and you should shout it from the rooftops.

Quick Actions
Come up with a USP for your business using this process.

Obtain feedback from your customers and fine-tune accordingly.

29: Position your expertise

An expert is a person who has a high level of skill and knowledge in a particular area. Experts are often thought of as the best problem solvers, solution providers or thought leaders – their knowledge is trusted by others.

Promoting yourself as an expert is an excellent way to gain trust and recognition in your industry. Customers love experts and would rather pay more for the product or service from someone who is known as one of the best in the business.

Imagine if you were thinking of franchising your business. Who would you rather take advice from – a franchising expert or a generalist? Who would you be prepared to pay more for? Who would you be most likely to recommend to others seeking the same solution? The expert wins every time.

When you focus upon a specific niche area and position yourself as an expert, you will most likely find yourself being called to deal with the same problems over and over again. After a while, you will find yourself able to create a set of solutions which can be applied to 90 per cent of these problems. Consequently, you will build up more and more references and testimonials, which will grant you more authority.

Over time, this creates a virtuous circle. Once people regard you as somebody who understands their needs, with proven methods and ideas, they will buy your services confidently.

However, many people are afraid to specialise, and instead pride themselves on being able to provide their clients with anything and everything.

Quick Questions

Are you an expert already? Ask yourself:

What are your greatest talents and skills?

What are the most important problems you solve?

What advice do people come to you for?

What have you been asked to speak about at conferences?

What kind of expertise do your clients value?

What level of expertise is expected in your business?

How can you prove your expertise?

Quick Win

Specialisation requires concentration and commitment. Creating an expert status in the marketplace calls for a particular strategy.

Here are some of the things you can do to position and promote your expert status:

- Make sure you are passionate about your area of expertise

- Make sure you know as much as you possibly can about it – become a guru on the subject

- Describe yourself as an expert or specialist in what you do

- Get a book published – claim the space and get yourself talked about as the thought leader in this area

- Write and publish White Papers on your specialist subject

- Offer talks in your expert area

- Offer your services as the resident on panels at conferences or events

- Run seminars and workshops educating others in your area of expertise

- Join associations and professional institutes that verify your expert status

- Keep up to date with all the latest thinking about your expert area.

Quick Success

Paul, Alan and Stephen are all portfolio FDs working within a group. Their role involves them working with a number of businesses as finance directors. Initially, they struggled to attract clients, owing to the strong competition in their market.

Following our mentoring sessions, they started to position themselves as specialists in their respective areas: Paul was an expert in the biotech industry; Alan in the restaurant trade; and Stephen in recruitment.

Almost immediately, their experience in niche areas made attracting clients far easier. This in turn gave rise to case studies and testimonials which they were able to share with potential clients, making it much easier for their alliance and referral partners to source good opportunities for them.

Quick Actions

Think about what you are already an expert in.

Start calling yourself an expert, or a specialist, and notice the response of your customers.

Use the word 'expert' or 'specialist' in your LinkedIn description.

30: Get your key messages right

'Find the value in your service and communicate it clearly.'

Your key messages are statements about your business, which resonate with your customer's needs. They should motivate and inspire, rather than simply inform. The messages you communicate to your market need to match the value you promise to deliver. Your key messages should focus upon what your product or service does for your customers, rather than merely a description of what it is.

For example, a creative print and design business offers printing, brochure design, branding, direct mail and email marketing.
Value message: the delivery of a variety of creative marketing solutions which will help you to attract good quality leads.

A photographer offers: commercial photography, publicity photographs and team pictures.
Value message: making an impact on your audience, creating the right impression, doing the business justice, and communicating the human side.

An accountant offers: end-of-year accounts, business and tax advice.
Value message: helping you to pay the right amount of tax at the right time, avoiding investigations. Giving you

peace of mind knowing that everything is taken care of by a trusted expert.

Your messages can be used in your marketing collateral on your website, in your verbal communication and on your social media. You may need a snappy strapline or positioning statement as a core message for your brand as well as some key message statements you can use in a variety of contexts.

The clearer you are about the value you offer, the more able you will be to influence your potential customers positively. To have the greatest chance of success, your messaging should be targeted at the specific needs and interests of your target audience.

Quick Questions
What value do you offer your customers?

What do they value most about your service or product?

Quick Win
To create your key messages you will need to ask yourself what your product or service ultimately does for your customers. You will need to 'hunt the value you give' by looking at your business through the eyes of your perfect customer.

Here are some questions you can ask yourself to find out what your service 'does', as opposed to what it 'is':
What do your customers say they really value about your services/product?

For each of the services you offer, what is the end result for what the client wants?

How will your clients benefit as a result of using your service?

Why do these things matter to them?

What words or phrases could inspire?

If you study your client testimonials, you will see certain phrases and statements that clearly describe the value of your service. It could be a very worthwhile investment to engage a professional copywriter to create your key messages.

Quick Success

Nitesh is the MD of a renewable energy company which encountered difficulties following the gradual withdrawal of government tax incentives for his product.

Nitesh came to me for mentoring, and during the course of our sessions, we began to explore what his key messages were and what he was passionate about in his business. It became apparent that Nitesh was extremely concerned about making a difference to the environment and believed his products were essential to this process, so we began by articulating his personal values, as opposed to merely the monetary value of his products, whose competitive advantage had since been eroded.

By concentrating on what his products could do for his customers – align with their corporate responsibility statements, help with ISO procedures, be used in their marketing messages etc. – rather than what they cost, Nitesh was able to free up his thinking, and began to come up with creative ideas as to how to reposition himself.

He commissioned case studies from some of his valued clients (see Quick Win #34), and the positive feedback he received energised him, and helped him to push forwards with a new website and branding. This in turn led to Nitesh forming alliances with other green energy providers, to start writing a blog on his website, and to position himself as a hub of information on renewable energy solutions.

So, from having one key message on cost which had since been eroded, Nitesh now has a number of key messages based on what he can help his customers achieve and, in the process, has moved from a commodity provider to a seller of solutions.

Quick Actions

Review your key messages.

Consider using a professional copywriter to extract and write a set of messages that really communicate the value you offer.

31: Choose the right marketing methods to get leads

'The right channel to market needs to reach the right buyers and generate the right quality of leads.'

You need to seek out the right marketing methods for your business, but there are so many out there to choose from that it is easy to be overwhelmed by all the information, and consequently fail to take any action at all.

It is important to understand how each method works, and to appreciate how it could form part of your marketing strategy before you make any decisions about how to spend your marketing budget.

Poor planning will result in a lot of wasted time and effort.

Here is a list of the most common marketing methods:

- Telemarketing

- Websites

- Search engine optimisation ('SEO')

- Social media

- Apps

- Online advertising (e.g. Google)

- Hard copy advertising (newspaper and magazines)

- Directory advertising

- Radio advertising

- Email marketing

- Direct mail

- Conferences and events

- Webinars

- Talks and seminars

- Networking groups

- Marketing materials – brochures, flyers, banners

- Car and van livery.

Most businesses will use a combination of these marketing methods – you need to find the right mix for you.

Quick Questions

Which marketing methods are right for your business?

Which combination could achieve your marketing goals?

Quick Win

First, define what you want your marketing to achieve – write it down, and be specific.

Review each potential marketing method and then evaluate each of them based on the marketing goals you have just defined.

Evaluate what marketing collateral you think you may need to support these methods.

These questions could be useful when meeting any supplier or provider for a particular marketing method:

Could you quantify the results which others have achieved using this method?

What are the potential benefits and risks?

What are the required resources, investment and time required?

What realistic ROI can I expect?

Once you have this information, you should be in a position to put together a marketing plan using your chosen methods. Remember to test and measure your results.

Quick Success
Mark and Paul are owners of a garden landscaping business, servicing both a commercial and domestic client base. They wanted to increase the flow of customer enquiries for large domestic landscaping projects and to generate more commercial appointments with hotels and private nursing homes. They spent some time evaluating the marketing methods which would be most likely to generate these required results.

They hadn't undertaken much marketing in the past, and so were not sure what was going to work for them. They had a reasonably good website but were not getting the quantity and quality of enquiries they were looking for.

The methods they evaluated were as follows:

- Social media campaign

- SEO for both markets

- A new mobile website

- Joining a number of local networking groups

- Telemarketing for commercial appointments

- Marketing materials – flexible brochure with inserts

- Local magazine advertising with direct mail inserts for the domestic market

- Van livery.

They decided not to outsource social media, but to undertake that themselves – one of the directors booked himself on to a course.

An SEO expert was deemed to be worth investing in, based upon his success with other businesses similar to theirs.

The mobile website was put on hold since this wasn't a priority.

They chose networking groups with a strong referral potential.

Three different telemarketing companies were consulted, and in the end they decided on a test campaign with the one they felt best understood their needs.

A designer and copywriter were engaged to put together a flexible brochure that could work as a standalone hard-copy, a page-by-page insert, or a flyer for direct mail.

They decided upon a targeted direct mail campaign for the domestic market, supported by a regular advert in the local village magazines.

Van livery was deemed essential – all their branding and contact details were promoted on the side of their vehicles.

All in all, they put together a simple marketing plan, choosing a combination of methods which they felt were most likely to generate the quality of enquiries they required. They stuck to their budget and used external providers where they realised that they didn't have the expertise, or the time, to do it themselves.

Quick Actions

Evaluate a selection of marketing methods which you think could work for your business.

Decide upon what you can do yourself and what you should outsource.

Ask yourself sincerely whether you have time and resources necessary to set up and run this marketing method.

What will it cost you in terms of time and money to do this?

How will you measure your success?

32: Write a simple marketing plan

'Write a plan and make a commitment to success.'

Once you are clear upon your marketing goals and the methods most likely to achieve these goals, you need to set it all down in writing.

Your marketing plan is your opportunity to bring together, and to clarify, all your creative thoughts and ideas for promotion. It will represent your tangible commitment to your business, and enable you to stay focused and on track.

Quick Questions
Do you know what you want your marketing to achieve?

Have you got a plan for this?

Quick Win
If you are like many busy business owners out there, your marketing plan is probably all in your head and hasn't ever been committed to paper.

To make it easy for you, here is a simple structure for you to work from:

- Business description – who you are and what you do

- Market – a description of what is happening in your industry

- Competition – what they offer, their strengths and weaknesses

- Target area(s) – your target geographic locations

- Niches – your target specialist area and/or sectors

- Marketing objectives – what you want to achieve

- Marketing methods – list the appropriate channels to market

- The budget – how much you commit to spend on each activity

- The strategy – key 'how to' actions for each method

- Resources – the resources required to implement the strategy. Internal and external providers.

Quick Success

After being made redundant, Jan decided to follow her passion and start her own business as a foot care professional. During her twelve-month training programme, she attended one of my sales and marketing courses to ensure that she would be fully prepared when it came to launching her business.

She used the time on my course to think through every element of her marketing plan and commit it to paper. She clarified her best target client (# Quick Win 11) and the areas she wanted to work within close to her home base.

Jan researched the best marketing channels for her business, checking out her competition and the routes to market they were using. She decided upon her budget, what she wanted to spend it on, and what return she could expect from it.

She planned a strategy for each marketing method which she systematically implemented, measuring the results as she went along.

Throughout her training programme, she planned how she was going to get enough customers to make her business successful. The result was that within three months of qualifying, she had enough customers to give her business a very healthy start.

She continued to implement her marketing strategies for both winning and retaining customers and now, two years on, is so busy she has to turn customers away. Jan knows exactly which marketing methods work and can turn them on and off like a tap whenever required.

Jan is now investing in her own therapy room at home, in order to accommodate more customers and minimise her travelling time so she can become more efficient. I am absolutely certain she will have a queue of customers at her door for as long as she is running her business.

This all started with a simple marketing plan, and Jan now has a successful business full of happy customers, all with happy feet!

Quick Actions

Think through and write down your marketing plan using the format provided.

Record the marketing methods used, paying attention to time spent, costs incurred and results achieved.

Review this plan every six months.

33: Brief suppliers effectively

*'To simplify means to eliminate the unnecessary
so the necessary may be heard.'*

As a busy business owner, you may find that you will need to engage the help of a number of experts to deliver your sales and marketing activities. It makes more sense to out-source the elements of your marketing plan that you do not have the skills or resources to deliver yourself. Your time is better spent doing what you are best at.

The challenge is to find the right suppliers and trusting them to deliver the results that are important to you.

The success of your marketing strategy will depend upon the suppliers delivering to agreed deadlines and achieving agreed outcomes.

You may engage suppliers for telemarketing, branding, brochure design, social media, digital marketing, website building, copy writing, email marketing, newsletter, CRM (Customer Relationship Management Systems) and more besides.

To be effective, all of these suppliers, once engaged, will need to be properly briefed by you.

From my experience, many suppliers of marketing services need to be given very clear briefs and to be project-managed closely. You, or someone within your organisation, will need to manage them and the service they are providing for you.

Marketing service providers can only do a good job for you if you provide them with a clear brief. It can be frustrating for suppliers if you are not clear with what you want and keep changing the brief. This can be costly and time-consuming for both parties.

If you use suppliers, make sure you have a clearly defined and agreed brief. You will be able to refer back to this brief and check that all the elements have been delivered. Your brief acts as a guide for the project and a referral point in the event of any disputes.

Quick Questions
Have you had any experiences when suppliers have not delivered to the standard you expected but had no brief to refer to?

Do you brief your suppliers effectively?

Quick Win
The specific detail of your briefs will vary according to the suppliers you are engaging. However, here are some guidelines to help you to structure your briefing conversations:

What do you want to achieve?

What are your objectives/measurable goals for the project?

What are your timescales and deadlines?

Who is going to manage the project?

Who are you targeting? Who is this aimed at?

What ideas and input do you have for the project?

What information do you need to provide the supplier and in what format?

Who is going to provide that information?

What are the stages of the project?

What is the review process?

What reporting or management information do you require and in what format?

What are the terms and conditions of engagement?

What insurance or guarantees of delivery do you have?

What is the process for changing the brief?

If the suppliers you engage are professionals, they should provide you with a scope of work, a delivery plan and a contract. You will have to sign off your agreement before they start. It is important that you brief them effectively to enable them to deliver for you, and for you to deliver on your obligations to them.

I have seen website and brochure design projects being held up for months because the client has not provided the content within the agreed deadlines. The clearer you are from the outset and the better the project can be managed between you and your supplier, the more likely you will be able to achieve the results you want.

Quick Success

I have had the experience of working with a number of suppliers of marketing services over my years in business, and get on best with the ones who effectively manage me through the process, and keep the project on track.

I, like you reading this book, am a busy business owner and outsource a number of services which I don't have the expertise to deliver myself. I haven't got the mental space to deal with all the technical elements of digital marketing and the pace and details of social media, so it is easier for me to outsource these services. I appreciate it when my suppliers take control and look after my interests. The ones that take a full brief, explain the process and expectations clearly and provide relevant updates without any chasing are ideal. I do appreciate my suppliers keeping things simple and clear and not overloading me with too much detail.

Once I have a supplier I can trust fully, I will keep using them. It is good to have a number of trusted suppliers who look after you and the delivery of your marketing strategy.

Our team of approved delivery partners in Heart of Business supports the needs of many of our mentoring clients, and all deliver to these standards (see www.heart-of-business.co.uk/approveddeliverypartners).

Quick Actions

Review your briefing process for suppliers.

Assess the success of your stable of suppliers.

Refresh and change the suppliers who are not delivering according to your brief.

34: Promote success

*'Sharing success builds credibility and showcases
achievement – it is a win-win for both parties.'*

A success story or case study is a description of a piece
of business you have carried out for one of your
customers. It acts as a practical example of work you
have undertaken which has achieved positive results for
satisfied customers.

Case studies are powerful because they relate to real
people, real experiences and real results. Publishing case
studies can help both you and your clients – you can help
to build your clients' profile, as well as offering an added
bonus for doing business with you.

Case studies make ideas tangible and can motivate those
business owners who relate to it, to take action.

They can be promoted on your website, blog, or
through your social media activities, discussed with
clients, or shared as examples when delivering talks
or workshops.

You can use the case study in its entirety, pick out headline
testimonial quotes, or present an abridged version – whatever suits your style best.

Case studies and testimonial quotes are extremely valuable

marketing tools, since they communicate the strongest possible success message about your business, providing real-life proof of the value you offer.

Quick Questions

How many case studies do you have that you can use to promote success?

Would it be useful to have some more?

Quick Win

Case studies

The first thing that is important here is to make sure that your case studies are written with the reader in mind. It is important to give them structure and share the customer's journey in a positive way.

Simple structure of a case study

Brief description of the business – who they are and what they do

The problems, challenges, needs the client had before using your service/product

Action taken

What the service/product helped to achieve

The results/impact on the business/bottom line

Where the business is now.

To view some examples of case studies written in this format, and promoted, go to http://www.heart-of-business.

co.uk/case-studies/client-cases.html and www.jackie-jarvis.
co.uk/case-studies/client-cases.html

How to get your case study or testimonial quotes
You will need your customer's permission to promote
their journey with you and ideally it would be good to
have their input into the creation of it. The main challenge
is getting this information from them. Like everyone they
are usually busy and writing may not be one of their skills.

The best way to obtain a case study is to extract what you
need verbally from the client, get it written up yourself,
and then have it signed off by the client. It may be advisable to engage an expert to write it.

You can also go to your clients at any stage of their time
working with you and ask for feedback. By asking a selection of appropriate questions, you can extract some
comments that would be valuable to use as stand-alone
quotes. Just ask your clients for permission to use it in
your publicity.

You can build up a library file of these testimonial quotes
by getting into the routine of asking for one each time you
come to the end of a job.

Once you have the case study and testimonial quotes you
will need to consider the opportunities you have to use
them and make a plan.

It is important to keep the case study up-to-date and fresh.
It needs to be representative of your current portfolio.

Quick Success

David and Matt have built up a product centred on the gathering and writing up of case studies. They found that the majority of businesses have loyal customers, but all too often fail to harness the positive feedback generated by these customers. This is because the businesses are either too embarrassed to ask, too modest to promote their successes, or simply too busy to undertake the process of translating verbal goodwill into engaging copy.

Their product involves interviewing their clients' customers for feedback and providing a detailed report which includes, amongst other things, testimonials, case studies and referrals.

Interestingly, customers are usually flattered to be included in case studies, and are subsequently only too happy to be asked about referrals. The most common feedback David and Matt received in this respect was 'I'd be happy to refer Company X – it's just that I'd never been asked before.'

However, to be powerful and credible, a case study must be authentic, and usually the only way this happens is to call the person to extract the key message verbally . . . which is why case studies are so often either badly written or avoided altogether!

For example, a common hurdle many business mentors have to overcome is in quantifying the value they provide, since many business owners are wary of committing money upfront for an outcome which cannot be precisely defined.

So, I identified some clients for David to call, and in the course of a telephone interview, by talking to the clients about how I had helped them, he was able to guide them towards articulating the value I provided, and draw out how they really felt about what I offered – something they would never have been able to do when writing an email on their own.

Hence, rather than bland case study quotes such as 'Jackie is great', I received excellent feedback from long-standing clients such as:

'Every time I meet my mentor, she really gets my brain going – afterwards I feel like I'm ready to climb Kilimanjaro.'

'If I had to put a figure on it, we're probably better off an additional £200,000 a year.'

Quick Actions
Make a commitment to have six case studies written for your business.

Put them on your website and promote them in your social media.

Start sharing your success stories when you present your business to potential clients.

35: Test and measure ROI

'If 50 per cent of your marketing is working, which 50 per cent is and which isn't?'

Testing and measuring the results from your marketing activities allows you to generate tangible facts and figures with which to support your future marketing plans. This will enable you to go beyond a 'gut feel' or 'suck it and see' approach.

If you do not record this information, you have no way of determining the most effective marketing method for any given activity. After all, how can you fine-tune your strategy to improve results if you don't know what they were in the first place, or decide what methods to drop and what to repeat? Ultimately, evaluating your return on investment (ROI) should be a must for any serious business owner.

You will need to set up a simple system to test and measure each of your marketing activities. You will require discipline to operate your system until you have gathered enough information to come to meaningful conclusions.

Some marketing methods are easier to evaluate than others, such as direct response marketing: e.g. targeted email campaigns, telesales or magazine response adverts. Other methods are harder to quantify, such as brand awareness marketing, relationship building or PR.

However, remember that many customers need to come into contact with a variety of your marketing messages, communicated via a number of channels over a period of time before they decide to buy from you.

Quick Questions

Do you know which of your current marketing methods is the most effective?

Can you identify the source of the majority of your new enquiries?

Quick Win

Decide how you will test and measure each marketing method prior to starting. You will need a system of recording all this information – a simple spreadsheet is all you need.

Test on a smaller scale first

If you are planning a direct mail campaign, test it on a small targeted group first, and count the responses before sending out a larger batch. This way, you will have a chance to fine-tune your approach, trying out different headlines, offers or calls to action.

Choose the right measure for the right method

The measure you choose should be easy to monitor and appropriate for the marketing method used. For example, you can set up different codes or reply references for direct mail campaigns, or you may monitor replies via a special reply email address.

Ask people where they heard about you

Asking people where they first heard about your business is probably the easiest and most immediate way to obtain answers. Get everybody in your organisation to gather this information. It can be done on the telephone when you receive an enquiry, in casual conversation whilst out and about, or formally at the end of a customer transaction. This information needs to be recorded, collated and evaluated.

Review your statistics

For online marketing, there is a wealth of ready-made statistics available: Google analytics can help to evaluate your website traffic, or mailing programmes can automatically check opening rates for newsletters and emails. Drill down, and find out what people are reading and responding to.

Evaluate results and make decisions

Once you have defined your marketing objectives and established your measuring system, you will be able to confirm the effectiveness of marketing activities. If they are not working as you hoped, you can fine-tune, try different approaches, or take the decision to end the activity early, and preserve your budget.

Quick Success

The new franchisees of a renewable energy company are given a marketing plan upon joining, along with a series of templates to use when running direct mail and advertising campaigns in their territories. Although all these campaigns have been tried and tested by Head Office, there is no absolute guarantee of success across different parts of the country, given varying demographics and personal needs.

Part of the learning curve for each individual franchisee is in the testing and measuring of the various marketing methods, coming up with a success formula for their region in the process.

When they run a direct mail campaign, they have to review the number of calls they receive, the quality of the leads, and the conversion of leads into customers. They have to work out how many sales are required in order to break even on the campaign and how many they need to make a profit.

Relatively speaking, direct mail campaigns can be expensive, and represent a risk for the franchisees, as some areas do better than others. Other marketing methods in the plan given to the franchisees include paid-for leads, Google advertising, exhibitions, country fairs, local advertising, networking, alliance partners, telemarketing, community events and referrals from existing customers.

The franchisees continue to learn and pay close attention to the results they get from each marketing method, to ensure that they generate a return on their investment.

Quick Actions

Set up a system for recording your marketing results.

Evaluate it on a month-by-month basis.

If a method does not work after thorough testing and fine-tuning, cut it!

Quick Wins to Make Your Marketing Work

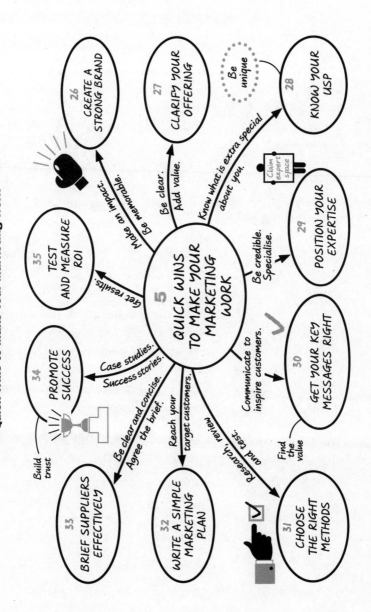

CHAPTER 6:
Quick Wins to Sell Effectively Without Being Pushy

36: Learn to love selling

*'Change the way you think about selling,
and the way you sell will change.'*

If the idea of selling makes you feel uncomfortable, it is likely that the sales calls you should be making will stay at the bottom of your priority list.

Many people hate the idea of selling, but love the idea of someone benefiting from the service or skills they have to offer. Deep down, we would all like to be ourselves whilst being successful at selling our products or services.

Thoughts that can block the 'love':

'I'm not an extrovert, so I can't sell'

'People hate being sold to'

'If I try to sell, I might be rejected'

'Selling is difficult and I don't like it'.

To learn to love selling, you must first start thinking about selling in a new way. You don't have to be an extrovert or pushy to succeed in sales – you can stay true to your 'authentic' self and still be successful.

To start with your thoughts about selling will influence how you feel and how you act, and these thoughts are a result of your own personal experiences, be they good or bad.

Quick Questions
How do you think about selling? Do you love it or hate it?

What thoughts do you have that may be blocking your love of it?

Quick Win
Take the focus away from yourself for a second, and think about how your product or service benefits your customers.

Selling is all about helping individuals make a decision that is right for them. If you enjoy helping people, you can enjoy selling in the same way. Think about it like this, and turn negative thoughts into positive ones – the better you are at selling, the easier it will be for your customers to buy from you, and the more you can help them.

Quick Success
Reg is the director of a company that produces promotional videos. As soon I started working with Reg, I noticed how proud he was of the quality of his videos and the service he was able to offer. He loved telling me stories of the projects he had been involved with and how pleased his customers had been with the results.

The thing was that Reg wanted more customers but he wasn't comfortable with selling. He kept making excuses to avoid any kind of prospecting activity, and was even reluctant to make contact with past clients.

It was all down to his negative beliefs about selling – Reg thought that to do it well he had to be pushy, and he didn't see himself in that way.

I worked with Reg over several sessions to shift the beliefs that were blocking his 'love' of selling. In particular, I encouraged him to focus on how much he could help his customers promote themselves.

One month, I set Reg the task of contacting eight previous customers, to investigate whether there was anything new that he could help them with. Ray was able to suspend his negative belief that follow-up calls were 'pushy' and made those eight calls. The results were that four customers were out, three didn't have any immediate needs but were very grateful for Reg's call, and one placed an initial order for £8,000 that eventually turned into a £40,000 project.

Once Reg saw these Quick Wins, he was able to shift his perspective, becoming more open to learning how to structure his sales conversations in order to help his customers buy from him.

Quick Actions

Jot down who has loved your product service the most in the past.

Note how you help your customers.

Suspend any negative beliefs and do what Reg did – call eight previous customers to find out if they need any help.

37: Understand what people love to buy

*'Help your customer achieve what they want and
you will achieve what you want.'*

When people buy products and services, what are they
really buying? It is not so much about the product or service
itself, as about fulfilling an outcome. People buy outcomes.

A buying decision can be made to satisfy a positive, or
avoid a negative, outcome, since people move either
towards pleasure or away from pain.

Examples of outcomes, negative and positive:

- Avoidance of worry

- Confidence boost

- Self-respect

- Avoidance of losing money

- Time-saving

- Freedom

- Prestige

- Protection

- Organisation

- Making progress

- Fear of getting left behind

- Being more effective.

Quick Questions
What was the last item or service you purchased for your business?

What outcome were you looking for (from the list above)?

Quick Win
Buying decisions are motivated by what is important to a particular person, and this is connected to their personal values. A personal value is something that matters deeply to a person – it creates mental filters which are used to seek satisfaction when choosing a product or service.

If you can uncover the fundamental outcomes and values that your customers are looking for, you will have much greater influence in your sales conversations.

Spot the difference between these approaches:

One bank clerk says, 'Open a savings account'; the other says, 'Plan for a secure future'.

One IT consultant says, 'Install Office 365'; the other says, 'Become more efficient and save time and effort'.

One FD says, 'Get help with a business plan'; the other says, 'Get help making more money'.

Which one is more motivational? The one that is feature-based, or the one that is outcome-based?

Quick Success

Steve was a talented website designer who took a great deal of pride in his work. He was asked to pitch for a piece of work from a marketer.

At the initial meeting, Steve spent a lot of time talking about the format, the colour scheme, and all the bells and whistles he could add to the website to make it as attractive as possible from a design perspective.

He was surprised to see that his customer was not as engaged as he thought she should be at this point. So he asked her what was most important to her about the website. Her answer was revealing and gave him the information he needed to win the business.

What she said was that she needed the website to generate results. It wasn't so much about it looking 'pretty' as about it being a marketing machine that could convert visitors into enquiries and sales.

It may well have been that the website Steve intended would have both looked good and operated as the marketing machine that his customer wanted. However, to motivate his potential customer to buy, he first needed to focus on the outcome that mattered most to her.

Quick Actions

Add these questions to your sales conversations and listen to the answers. Ask your customers:

What outcomes do you want?

What is most important to you when making an investment in a particular product or service?

Make sure you use the outcomes and values the customer tells you about in your description of what your product or service does. You will instantly make your description of your product or service more appealing.

38: Make a connection

*'Be present with people and you will build
better relationships.'*

People are more likely to buy from somebody they like
and trust. Most of us make our minds up about a person
within a few minutes of meeting them. The quicker you
can make a connection with a person in a sales situation,
the more open they will be both towards you and to what
you have to offer.

A connection can be thought of as a feeling of comfort, or
rapport. You can influence this connection as you build
trust – your integrity is a key ingredient.

Quick Questions

Recall a time when you were aware that you did
not connect with someone in a business context. What
happened as a result?

Recall a time when you did connect with someone in a
business context. How did that influence events?

Quick Win

Since much of our communication is non-verbal, we are
often unaware of the messages we send out to the people
we meet. Our body language and voice tone will influence
how our verbal communication is interpreted.

If you have a positive intention towards the person with whom you are communicating, it is most likely to be transmitted non-verbally as well. If your feelings are negative, it is very difficult to hide that in your body language and tone of voice.

Giving a person your undivided attention and being fully 'present' when you are with them is most likely to give them a positive experience. Being 'present' means being fully engaged and focused. In giving someone your full attention, you are communicating the message that both they and their time are important. This goes a long way towards making a positive connection.

Being open to learning about the person you are meeting, with no judgements or preconceived ideas, will also help you to connect. The less of a barrier you put up when you meet somebody, the more likely you will be to engage positively with them, and the more likely they will be to feel comfortable with you.

Be open and curious about getting to know who they are and what is important to them. Be conscious of the level of rapport you are able to build. Pace the situation and take your time – the rapport will build as you get to know the person better.

Quick Success
During a sales coaching day with Steve, a renewable energy consultant, we had an appointment with a farmer who was interested in an alternative heating solution for his home, since he was not connected to the electricity grid.

The home in question was a ramshackle farmhouse at the end of a long dirt track. However, Steve did not jump to any conclusions. When he met the farmer and his wife, he gave them his full attention and listened intently. He was there to help them.

The farmer and his wife were both on their guard and obviously wary – it transpired that they had previously had a number of negative experiences with sales representatives from various energy companies. As Steve listened and acknowledged their concerns, they began to talk more openly and shared some of these negative experiences.

I watched how Steve engaged with them and showed a real interest in both them and their story. At the end of the meeting they told Steve they had cash savings to hand to buy his heating system and would be keen to take the next step.

Quick Actions

Make a decision to be 100 per cent present in all your sales meetings – leave all thoughts about anything other than the person you are with behind. Notice the impact.

Think about the connections you have with the people you meet – notice when it is good and when it isn't. Be aware.

39: Uncover clients' pain and desires

'Pain is an indication of weakness that needs to leave your business. Desire is necessary to motivate that change.'

A key element of any successful sales conversation is being able to uncover your prospect's challenges, frustrations, needs and desires.

If you do that well, you will help your prospect to clarify what they want and what they don't want. This clarity helps to motivate the person to take action, be it moving away from pain or towards pleasure.

Once you uncover the gaps between where your prospect is now and where they want to be, they are more likely to be open to your solution.

Quick Questions
What questions would uncover your prospects' problems?

What questions would uncover their needs?

Quick Win
It is worth spending the time creating a really good list of questions to uncover challenges and priorities for your prospect to focus on.

Here are some useful exploratory questions, which you can adapt to your product, service or particular situation:

What is the biggest frustration you are currently facing?

What are the main problems you are experiencing?

What impact is this having on your business?

What is it costing you?

What are the risks leaving things as they are?

What would you like to be different?

What have you tried already?

What help do you think you need?

What do you most want to achieve?

What matters most to you?

What are your priorities?

What would be your best result?

What would be the perfect solution for you?

What do you want this to do for your business?

What are your timescales?

If you asked a handful of these questions in any sales conversation, then kept quiet and listened carefully, the answers would provide an excellent steer for how to position your offering. The more you know about your prospect's pain and desires, the better placed you will be to help.

Exploring the 'real' issues requires a degree of trust and rapport-building – there is an art to guiding somebody so that they tell you what they really want and need help with. It is sometimes not the most obvious points that matter the most.

Quick Success

John is a cash flow consultant and found that when he had opportunities to engage new clients, questioning and listening were the most important tools he had to both diagnose the problems and design the solution.

As John really believed his role was to help his clients, he knew it was impossible to do that without first asking the right questions. But what were the right questions?

He found himself floundering a bit during his early sales conversations. He wasn't quite sure how to ask the right questions to uncover the problems, establish needs or how to control the conversation so that he wasn't overwhelmed with the customer's detail.

Over time he learnt to control the conversations better by guiding the discussions from problems and towards outcomes, establishing the gaps that needed filling along the way. He used to summarize and clarify what he was hearing, to make sure he had got it right, and the impact was that he received more and more agreement. And that was before he told them anything about what he did.

Now he is practised at the art and finds he can softly lead sales conversations in the right direction for both him and his potential clients. It was worth taking the time to really think about the right questions to uncover the real issues for the client.

Quick Actions

Try out the exploratory questions in this chapter with a potential client.

Summarize the pains or desire you hear, and gain agreement from the client before you move on to describe your offering.

Notice the impact of this approach. Executed well, it will be a positive experience for both parties.

40: Talk the customer's language

'We all talk our own language and make our own meanings.'

Speaking the same language doesn't mean that we all understand or interpret information in the same way. We have our own history, experiences and values which all influence our choices.

Using too much industry jargon or technicalities will not be helpful in providing your customer with the clarity they need in order to buy. If you are aware of how another person communicates and can adapt your style and language to suit them, you will build a better rapport and increase understanding.

Words are one way in which we express ourselves, and if you can mirror the words your customer uses when explaining what they want, you will add power and clarity to your communication.

Quick Questions

How aware are you of the words people use to describe what they want?

How aware are you of the words you use to describe your solution?

Have you got into the habit of using too much technical or industry jargon, which leaves your customers confused?

Quick Win

Step into your customers' shoes and 'talk their talk'. Start paying attention to how your prospects and customers express what they want. You may hear certain points being emphasised again and again.

Write down some of these key words – make sure you get them right.

In subsequent sales conversations, with these prospects or customers, use as many of these keywords as possible – you will notice that they visibly relax, nod, or tell you 'That's right'.

Talking the customer's language gives a very strong message of care and understanding.

Quick Success

I remember a time when I was coaching a member of my own team, Amanda, to sell effectively. She was listening to one of my sales consultations with a potential client.

Before the consultation we had asked the customer to complete a questionnaire, and before each consultation we read the questionnaire so we had an understanding of the business and could use some of the words the customer used to describe his situation. One of the calls I made to demonstrate the process was to a steel manufacturer.

I recall Amanda laughing when she heard me talk about selling more steel a lot during the call. She knew I didn't know anything about steel. The point was he did, and all

I had to do was repeat back to him what he wanted in his language.

I did end up helping this steel manufacturer as he bought a place on the nine-month sales and marketing fast-track programme we were running at the time.

He learnt exactly how to sell more steel!

Quick Actions

Next time you are having a sales conversation, be more aware of your customers' language.

Jot down some key words and use them when you summarize and when you talk about your solution.

Convert any technical or industry jargon into simple terms.

Talking your customers' language is an art and to do it well you need to listen and care enough to explain things in a way that means the most to them.

41: Deliver the solution match

*'Your customers care about results and solutions,
so help them to achieve what matters most to them.'*

Your sales proposition should be a solution to a problem or a need. A solution aims to solve the pain or desires which you have uncovered during the exploratory part of your sales conversation. The sales proposition outlining your solution may take the form of a presentation, a dialogue or both.

A solution match occurs when a connection or link is made between what is important to your prospect and what you are able to fulfil. This is about telling or showing a customer exactly what your solution will do for your prospect and explaining all the elements of the solution in a way that means most to them.

It is about making a fit. The better the fit is communicated, the more chance there is of a positive reaction.

To make the solution match effectively, you will need to be very clear about the elements and benefits of your solution. Listening and asking the right questions are vital parts of any sales conversation, prior to any solutions being offered.

Without having the correct information about your prospects' needs, problems or values, it will be impossible to make the match. You will also need to be flexible and able to communicate what you do for people in different ways.

Quick Questions
When you have sales conversations with prospects, how closely are you matching your solution to their exact needs, problems or values?

How aware are you of making a fit between what they want and how you describe your solution?

Quick Win
Here are the simple steps to improve your solution-matching with any sales conversation:

Summarize your prospect's problems and desired outcomes – gain agreement and show you have heard what matters to them.

Confirm their issues – highlight their values and what they want going forward.

Explain your proposition for them using their language – link back to what this solution will do for them and for their business.

Use visual aids to help your solution make sense.

Share examples of how you have helped similar organisations in the past.

Explain how you and your company work best to achieve outcomes for your clients.

Set positive expectations going forwards for when you work together.

Quick Success

My own experience of how well this approach can work was when I visited a company along with my partner to discuss the provision of social media services to our company, Heart of Business.

To the older generation, social media can be overwhelming and rife with jargon. However, Julia was both friendly and professional, immediately giving a very positive first impression. She kept things simple, concentrating upon our aims for our company's social media activities. She asked lots of probing questions, and then demonstrated visually how her company worked and what they could potentially do for us.

Julia reflected our language and our values in describing what her company could do for us.

I felt a sense of peace at that meeting – something which is familiar to me when I sense that someone is going to do a good job, and look after us well, so it was easy to say 'Yes'.

Quick Actions

Practise tailoring your pitch to fit with what each individual wants from you.

Use visual aids or relevant success stories to explain your proposition.

Be aware of how your prospects respond to your pitch. Notice when you are 'matching' and when you are not.

42: Position your value along with your price

'Believe you are worth the price you charge and the results you help to achieve.'

Communicating your price or fees can be the most difficult part of the whole sales process.

> What are you worth?
>
> What is your service worth?
>
> How do you justify your rates or prices?

Pricing can be a strange thing – it has a strong influence on how you feel about the value of what you provide. If you undercharge, you may end up working very hard for little reward, being perceived as cheap and therefore not so valuable. With lots of work but no time to develop your business or your skills, you may get stuck at a level from which you find it hard to escape.

Overcharging can be equally problematic. You may either price yourself out of the market, or find yourself under such intense pressure to justify your rates that it affects your delivery.

Either way, it is vital to find the right balance for both you and your customers. You need to feel comfortable about the price you charge your customers and your customers need to feel comfortable about the value they perceive themselves to be receiving.

Quick Questions
How comfortable do you feel when you relate your prices to your customers?

Do you believe the price you charge is in line with the value you offer?

Quick Win
A primary objective for your sales conversation is to establish your value to your customers.

How to position your value with your price
Establish the potential impact of your product or solution for your client's business – this may be expressed in terms of additional sales, profit, efficiency or quality.

Guide the conversation towards those results. What are they hoping it will achieve for them?

Manage expectations to avoid over-promising in order to win the business.

Agree a 'scope of work' for the price you are quoting – otherwise, 'scope creep' can become a significant issue.

Back up your value with a relevant success story or case study that demonstrates the value you have been able to deliver for others. Have these successes written up.

Value and price need to balance. Your customer should be confident that they can benefit from the promised results and it is an investment worth making.

Quick Success

Sara runs a virtual assistant ('VA') business and employs a small team of people. She joined my sales and marketing academy for six months in order to learn how to win more clients, as she had been having some challenges presenting her prices to customers and closing deals.

Sarah had made a decision to position her VA business at the higher end of the market. Hence, it was vital for her to explain the additional value a client would receive, since there were cheaper VA services around.

Sarah managed a highly skilled team who were all capable of dealing with the usual business-owner requirements of administrative, marketing and book-keeping services.

The biggest benefit that Sarah offered was that she managed and trained her team of VAs and had the systems and processes in place to run an extremely efficient practice.

Clients would not have the stress of managing their VA and would have the security of knowing that whatever they needed, someone in the team could do it. There would also always be someone there to cover sickness or holiday. The client would never be left managing on their own.

Sarah had to obtain agreement in her sales pitches on the additional value her team offered, which would justify the higher hourly rate. Once she learnt the right way to do this, her confidence and sales conversion rates soared.

Quick Actions

List the value you offer for the prices you charge.

Write up case studies that demonstrate this value in tangible terms.

Obtain testimonials for these case studies, which emphasise the value you offer.

43: Close softly

*'You can sell without selling, and close comfortably for
both you and the customer.'*

A sale is not 'closed' until the customer has agreed to pay
for your product or services. Depending upon your particular sales process, this may involve signing an agreement,
paying a deposit, setting up a standing order or paying in
full. The potential client has only finally stepped over the
line and become a customer when the fee has been paid.

Closing a piece of business which you have been working
on for some time is a good feeling. Depending on your
sales cycle, reaching that point may vary from minutes to
days or even years.

Many people become frustrated by the challenge of
'closing', especially if they find it uncomfortable to ask for
business. 'Closing softly' is all about taking small steps
towards securing the sale, whilst at the same time verify-
ing whether the client is likely to go ahead. This safeguards
against wasting undue effort and energy by hanging on to
too many 'maybes'.

Closing the sale is something that you need to always be
conscious of – unless you close, you don't get the chance
to deliver, and you don't get paid!

Quick Questions

How many potential clients do you have in your sales pipeline that you haven't closed yet?

How do you feel about closing sales? Do you find it easy or difficult?

Quick Win

To close effectively you need to go about it in a series of simple steps. The more you encourage a comfortable 'yes' as you go through the sales process with your clients, the easier it will be to close when you reach the point at which they are ready to go ahead. These are the steps at which 'yes' is the answer you need before proceeding:

The closing checklist

Is this person or business a good prospect for you? Do they have a need, problem or challenge that you have the resources and expertise to solve?

Depending on how they came into your sales pipeline, have they agreed to talk to you or meet with you and take your initial, no-obligation step to find out more?

After questioning, have they agreed to your summary of their problems/needs or challenges?

Have they agreed with your solution and the benefits you have presented?

Have they got the budget?

Have you scoped the work and presented the proposal?

Have they engaged with the value and agreed the price?

Have you got the agreement signed or confirmed by email?

Have they agreed the next step to move forward?

Do you have a start date in the diary?

Have you received payment?

Use these steps to build rapport and develop your relationship with your client. Closing the business should now become easy and comfortable for both parties.

Quick Success

When Matt first started his copywriting business, he had just come out of working in the corporate environment and wasn't used to working with small business owners. The challenge he had was getting the businesses who wanted his services over the line, deposits paid, and a timeline established to get started.

When he first started he was, like so many other start-ups, very grateful for the first few clients who said 'yes' to him. However, Matt didn't like to 'push' – he wasn't used to that and didn't want to risk losing clients by setting too many uncomfortable rules.

The situation that developed was that Matt received lots of 'I'd like to go ahead' answers, but getting the clients to the point where they paid a deposit and were ready to start was another issue entirely.

After working with me, Matt began to structure his sales process, making sure he obtained agreement at each step of the closing process. He found that this made matters far easier – he now didn't start work until he had a scope of work agreed and deposits paid in full.

He developed a professional client engagement process, which started teaching his clients how to work effectively with a copywriter.

He stopped wasting valuable time and energy on clients who didn't have the budget to pay for the quality of work he was able to deliver.

The result has been that Matt now feels comfortable closing the right kind of business and is working with clients who value his talent and ability.

Quick Actions

Go for 'NO' – get back to all your maybes and ask if they do want to go ahead.

Get agreement for a scope of work and ask for a deposit before you start work (if you don't do this already).

44: Care about follow-up

'Follow up opportunities promptly – it shows you care.'

It is vital to carry out follow-up, by telephone or email, after an initial contact. Follow-up is, without doubt, the most important sales activity.

Market research studies show that around 80 per cent of sales resulted from people who followed up at least five different times after the initial sales contact, before a customer said 'yes'. The same studies illustrate that 92 per cent of people will have given up after four 'no' answers, whilst only 8 per cent will ask for the order a fifth time.

Some people believe that following up is regarded as 'too pushy', whilst others find themselves too busy or too disorganised to do it properly. We are all very busy and your customers are no different. They may well be interested in your proposal, but they forget to respond, they become distracted by other issues, they fail to prioritise.

To follow up demonstrates that you are interested and acts as a reminder to your customer. Most people will thank you for following up – it shows you care and want their business.

Quick Questions
Do you have opportunities that you should have followed up but haven't?

Have you ever lost business because you didn't follow up?

Quick Win

To follow up properly, you will need to get into a routine. This will involve setting up a system and keeping the focus.

You will need:

An easy-to-use CRM system, spreadsheet, or card system, to keep your contacts and client notes in order.

Programme reminders so you don't forget.

The discipline to set some time aside each week – 'Follow-Up Friday' can be a great idea.

An easy-to-use diary – either on your phone, iPad or (for the older ones amongst us) in physical form.

Then you do need to do it! All the systems in the world won't make it happen – you need to. People value those who follow up, whether it's on a networking event, a meeting, a sales lead, a LinkedIn invitation, or following a referral.

It is good manners to acknowledge anybody who has made contact with you, especially where there may be an opportunity to further a business relationship. It does take time though, and you need to be organised.

Quick Success

I think follow-up is one of my own personal strengths – I take pride in making sure that I respond quickly and promptly to potential clients, business partners and all the other enquiries I receive. It does take time to do this, but I am reminded that when somebody does not follow up promptly with me, I immediately lose trust.

I once had an experience with a financial adviser who came to talk to me about my personal finances. We had a great meeting, I liked him, and he gave the impression that he was trying to look out for my needs.

I had already decided before he left that I would use his services. I told him that I was extremely busy, and that a quick bullet-point email to get the relevant paperwork to him would be greatly appreciated. He promised to do this immediately.

Had he done so, I would now be his client. I never did get my bullet-point email list, and therefore I never took the action I needed to get his help.

The lesson from this is to always do what you say you are going to do and follow up.

Quick Actions

Set up an organised follow-up system.

Follow up those you know you need to.

Set specific times in the week to follow up.

45: Personalise proposals

'Your proposal is your commitment to help your customers.'

A proposal is your summary of what your client will get for their money.

You should only usually prepare a proposal after you have already gained a conceptual agreement from your client, following an initial sales conversation. By this point, you should have already explored the client's problems, needs and budget.

Your proposal can be delivered in either electronic, hard copy or, ideally, in person, which gives you another chance to get in front of them. Your style of delivery will depend on your client's expectations, together with the nature and value of the work you are proposing.

Your client may wish to compare your proposal with others, so it is essential to put together a professional document. Your proposal will show your client how well you have listened and understood their position and requirements.

Quick Questions
How effective are your proposals?

Are they helping you to win business?

Quick Win

It is a good idea to create a basic proposal template which covers the key sections important to your proposal. You can add in the individual customer's detail later as required.

Section headlines that include the word 'your' will personalise your proposal template. Don't make your proposals too long; two to three pages is fine, and remember to keep the language straightforward and clear.

Here is a simple formula that you can follow:

Introduction – refer to your last meeting, along with an overview of what to expect in this proposal.

Situation – this is your summary of what you considered to be important at your last meeting. Remember to mirror your customer's language and priorities.

Objectives – bullet-point exactly what your customer has told you.

Solution – break this down so that the client can clearly see all the key elements. You may also choose to include standard descriptions of your service, product and methodology.

Value – make sure that you communicate the ultimate value of each element of the solution.

Price – outline your charges clearly.

Plan – include suggested targets and timescales.

Next step – detail the follow-up that you have agreed.

Sign-off – a positive statement about working together in the future.

Quick Success

When I was coaching David, from a company that supplied and maintained office plant displays, he admitted to often losing business after sending off his proposals. His sales conversations were good and he always built rapport with potential clients, but it seemed like his proposals were not hitting the mark.

We analysed why this might be, and asked some of his clients for their opinions. The feedback we received was that David's proposals were a) too long, which often meant they were put to one side; b) too wordy; c) not visual enough, and d) too standardised, with no personalisation.

David took my advice and made some major changes to his proposals. He started to include a summary of the client's objectives from the meeting, taking care to use the client's exact language. He also cut his proposals down from eight pages to a maximum of three, and introduced pictures of the plants he had suggested in order to make the proposals more visual.

The results were almost instantaneous. David started getting emails thanking him for his proposals and there was a measurable increase in the number of clients who agreed to go ahead with David's services.

Quick Actions

Examine your proposals critically – what could you improve?

Personalise your proposals by adding 'situation' and 'objectives' sections.

Ask your clients for feedback on your proposals – were they helpful or confusing?

Chapter Review

Quick Wins to Sell Effectively Without Being Pushy

6 — QUICK WINS TO SELL EFFECTIVELY WITHOUT BEING PUSHY

36 LEARN TO LOVE SELLING
- Be yourself and help customers.
- Change the way you think!

37 UNDERSTAND HOW PEOPLE BUY
- Pain / Pleasure
- Fulfil outcomes towards pleasure away from pain.

38 MAKE A CONNECTION
- Be present
- Build rapport quickly.
- Have a positive intention.

39 UNCOVER CLIENTS' PLAN AND DESIRES
- Motivate change.
- Questioning
- Listening

40 TALK THE CUSTOMER'S LANGUAGE
- Don't use jargon.
- Use your customer's words.

41 DELIVER THE SOLUTION MATCH
- Solve the pain.
- Fulfil the desire.

42 AGREE VALUE ALONG WITH PRICE
- £ + benefits
- Find the balance.

43 CLOSE SOFTLY
- Take small steps.

44 CARE ABOUT FOLLOW-UP
- Be prompt.
- Create a system.

45 PERSONALISE PROPOSALS
- Proposal template.
- Summarize individual needs.

CHAPTER 7:
Quick Wins to Build Team Talent and Support

46: Get the right people doing the right jobs

'When people do what they are good at and passionate about . . . results flow.'

Your business is only as good as the talent you have in it, so how do you capitalise on that?

The key is to make sure you have the right people doing the right jobs from the start. When you and your team members are able to focus on what they are best at, you will get more 'flow' in your business.

It starts with you being very clear about the roles in your business, and what talent, skill and personalities are needed to fill these roles in order to deliver results.

It is a common mistake to try and fit the person to the job – you often end up with somebody who struggles to achieve what is expected of them.

You will probably find that you and your fellow directors need to fulfil a number of roles during the early days of your business. You will, however, need to be clear about what roles will need filling in the long term, and have a plan to replace yourself when the time is right.

Quick Questions

Do you have the right people in the right roles?

Are you making the most of the talent you have in your business?

Quick Win

Have a clear organisational structure

No matter how big or how small your business, start by mapping out an organisational structure which shows key departments, job roles and reporting lines.

List the key functions in your business, such as:

- Operations

- Sales

- Marketing

- Administration

- IT

- Finance

It doesn't have to be complicated, but it does need to show who is responsible for which function . . . or which functions, as is the case in many small companies.

Write clear job descriptions

A job description is essential to help you visualise the person you want for the functions in your business. The mere act of creating a job description will provide you with a sense of clarity. It will also form the basis for the recruitment of the right person for any given position.

SAMPLE ORGANISATIONAL STRUCTURE

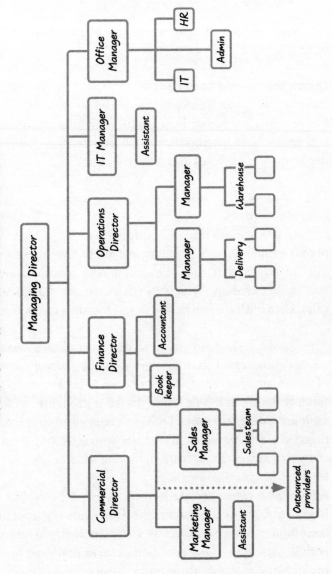

Here is a simple structure for a job description:

- Job title

- Job purpose (in one line)

- Key areas of responsibility

- Key tasks to be carried out

- Skills (essential and desired)

- Character (qualities and personality traits)

- Success measures

Interview with care

If you are conducting the interviews, make sure you prepare fully. Do not ask any old interview questions – ask questions that are relevant to the job description you've prepared and which will demonstrate that person's suitability both for the position and for your company.

Afterwards, follow up on references – it shows you are serious – and run a second interview with another member of your team, if appropriate. This could be backed up by personality profiling. Some examples of personality profiling tools are Talent Dynamics, DISC profiling and MBTI (Myers Briggs), which provides additional insight into a person's character, as well as likely strengths and weaknesses.

Start with a probationary period

Make sure you don't commit to a long-term contract until the employee has successfully completed a probationary period with you. Make sure you observe and review their performance during this period.

Positively induct into your business

How a new person starts work with your business dramatically influences their future performance, so make sure you plan and implement an induction process that gives them the best possible start. It doesn't matter how small your business is, an induction programme of some description is still vital.

Recognise and develop skill

Make sure that you make the most of the talent you already have in your business – regular performance reviews will help you to understand what each member of your team wants out of their career. Offer training and development to those who have the ability and aspiration to grow.

Quick Success

Selom, the MD of a company specialising in CRM systems, recruited a sales director as part of a new business growth strategy. He had decided that he needed to relinquish some of his control and responsibility for sales. A few months later, during the probationary period, he realised that the person he had chosen was not right for the position. Rather than carrying on and hoping for the best, or back-tracking and retaking the role of sales himself, he decided to re-recruit for the role. The position was simply too important to have the wrong person doing it.

After spending some more time reviewing the responsibilities and skills required for the role, and following further performance conversations with his team, Selom realised that there was already someone in his team who had the potential to succeed in the role. He ended up recruiting internally.

Selom realises that his business will only ever be as good as the team behind it, and that they are responsible for his company's most important value of 'putting the customer first'. Hence, making sure he has the right people for the right roles, developing their talent, and keeping them motivated are the most important growth strategies for the business. The highest monthly sales figures in twenty years have been the payback from his decision to recruit a sales director internally.

Quick Actions

Review your organisational structure – do you have the right people in the right roles?

Consider the talent you have in your business and ways to increase the 'flow' of that talent.

47: Learn to let go

'Freedom comes from trusting your team enough to take responsibility.'

When you have been the main driver of your business for many years, it can seem easier to carry on doing it all yourself rather than ceding any control.

To grow any business beyond being a sole trader, you will need the support of a reliable team and outsourced suppliers.

Many business owners struggle to do everything themselves, simply becoming busier and busier as their business grows. They struggle to delegate, afraid that if they give up any control, something will go wrong and they will lose the business they have struggled so hard to build. This usually results in the business being unable to grow.

A defining characteristic of a commercial business is that it can run effectively and profitably without the business owner in it. Think of it as a car, which could be driven by a different driver, or a machine which could be operated by someone other than the owner themselves.

If you, as a business owner, wish to build a business that you can sell or exit from at some point in the future, you will need to see it as a machine that can be operated without you.

You may be at a stage when you just want to be able to go away for a long holiday and leave your business and your team to run it. Or you may be feeling overwhelmed with the tasks you have to do yourself, and need to either outsource them or delegate them to a member of your team.

Either way, you know you need to let go, but are not sure where to start.

Quick Questions
What are you doing that you know you shouldn't be doing in your business?

What could you outsource to an expert?

What prevents you delegating?

Quick Win
Letting go is as much an attitude of mind as it is a business decision. It starts with you understanding yourself and what is stopping you from letting go.

Make a list of all the things that you are currently doing that you shouldn't be doing in your business, which you are hanging on to because there is no one else who you think can do them as well as you can.

Ask yourself which tasks you would really like to let go of. What is stopping you from doing so – fear, money, stress, time?

If you had the right person to do these tasks for you, what would you then be able to achieve?

What are your options – in-house team member; outsourced supplier; new recruit?

What do you need to have in place in order to let go?

Set up systems, structure and measures
When you have a system, structure and some key measures in place, you will be able to remain in control but have somebody else undertaking the delivery for you.

Provide a clear brief and review success
Make sure you brief fully and set up a feedback/review system to ensure that you can let go and trust that the work will get done in the way you need it to.

Quick Success
Over the years I have found it hard myself to let go of the tasks in my business which I should not have been doing, or didn't really have the skill to do. When I did let go, I was often one of those annoying micromanagers who tried to control things so much that it defeated the whole point of delegation.

I had had some bad experiences with the people I had recruited in the past, causing me more problems than helping me, as well as being let down by some of the suppliers I had trusted.

I often used to say that I always did better when I just relied on myself. I knew logically that I needed to work with a team, but trusting myself enough to pick the right people was the first hurdle I had to get over.

I followed my own advice and now have two business partners in Heart of Business and a team of approved delivery partners who we all fully trust to deliver successfully in their expert areas. We outsource our Heart of Business social media to a wonderful supplier who does a great job, both in managing us for content and driving the strategy. I have a super administration assistant, and a part-time marketing assistant who is so much better than I am with all the latest technologies!

It is often true that you teach best that which you most need to learn.

Quick Actions

Decide what you could let go of in your business.

Find the right person/supplier you trust to take it over.

48: Communicate expectations and motivate

*'The more clarity there is in your business,
the better your ability to achieve results.'*

The ideal for any business is to have a team which has the energy, enthusiasm and focus to make things happen. They possess a shared vision which inspires them, and are committed to the achievement of team goals. They feel important and valued members of a team; they pull together and are excited to be part of something that is growing and moving forwards.

The energy and enthusiasm of your team is vital to your productivity and to great customer service. A team that feels motivated will give more and achieve more. Their energy is the fuel which is needed to move your business forwards.

The clearer your team is about what you want from them, the more likely they are to be efficient, effective and creative. It is in your interest to ensure that you do everything you can to sustain their motivation and commitment. People will work harder and show more loyalty when they know what they are doing is appreciated, and they feel valued for their contribution.

It can be all too easy to take your team for granted and expect them to just do their job because you pay them to do it.

Your team members will be affected by the way you communicate your expectations to them – your clarity is essential. If you are constantly changing direction or sending out confused messages, your team's focus and motivation will be most likely to reflect that.

Quick Questions

How clear are your team members about what is expected of them?

How clear are you?

What do you do to motivate your team?

Quick Win

To create a team atmosphere that is a pleasure to be part of, you will need to be consistent, communicate clearly, and keep everyone motivated.

How to motivate your team

- Take time to share your vision for the business with them

- Involve the team in your planning process – remember people support that which they help to create

- Emphasise the importance of their role – be clear about what that role is and for what you want them to assume responsibility

- Explain tasks clearly and provide them with the relevant tools

- Help them to set meaningful goals and objectives

- Praise their hard work and achievement

- Recognise and reward results

- Provide an opportunity for healthy competition

- Thank individuals for their contribution

- Hold regular performance reviews

- Organise the occasional team social and have fun

- Provide learning opportunities

- Care and be flexible with their personal needs

- Remember the personal things that matter.

As the business owner, you are likely to be the natural team leader. Be aware of the impact that your communication style has on your team – is it inspiring? You have a huge influence over your team's levels of clarity and motivation – there is a lot you can do to make a big difference.

Quick Success

Stella runs a training business and has a small team who have been with her for a number of years. One of her team members – Tina – has the job of business development and the second team member – Kayleigh – is in charge of marketing. Stella was the kind of person who always enjoyed starting something new, and she was consequently often away either training, or planning the next programme, book or idea for the business.

Tina and Kayleigh were often left alone in the office trying to come up with new strategies and plans to attract more clients. However, they didn't really know what Stella wanted them to focus on. They would have meetings together when she came in to the office, and she did involve them in the planning process, but the problem was that Stella was so full of ideas that just when they had started to implement the agreed plan, Stella would come up with another new idea. Tina and Kayleigh sometimes found this counterproductive.

Stella realised that she needed to change things and asked her team to join her on some of the business mentoring sessions she was receiving.

Involving the team in this way gave them the opportunity to work together to create a fresh vision for the business, agree the breakthrough goals for the year ahead, and decide on exactly who they should be targeting for business.

Stella also made a commitment to stick to the plan they had agreed and Tina and Kayleigh decided to be more assertive and challenge potential changes to see whether they would in fact add value or whether they were simply diversions.

As a result of this involvement in the planning and decision-making process, they all now feel more motivated and valued. Most importantly, they all now have the clarity and focus they need to go forward and win the business they deserve.

Quick Actions

Think of a way of communicating your vision and goals to your team.

Consider what you could do to show how much you value their contribution.

49: Give feedback positively

'Feedback helps us all to grow.'

Giving feedback is an essential skill for any business owner. It can be used to develop and enhance your team's talent, whilst improving the ongoing delivery of your service.

Feedback is praising good performance, supporting effective behaviour, and guiding someone back on track when their performance is not meeting expectations. If the feedback is clear, it can help in understanding what 'good looks like', and also what the person needs to do to change for the better.

However, the challenge with giving and receiving feedback is that it is usually dreaded by both parties. It can be interpreted as criticism and the receiver often becomes defensive.

If you don't like confrontation, you may avoid giving critical feedback for fear of triggering bad feelings.

Think of it this way, though – if you don't give feedback when a member of your team has developed poor performance habits, you are not giving them a chance to rectify the situation.

Likewise, if you don't give feedback when someone is performing well, you are missing an opportunity to maintain high performance levels, and to inspire your team members reaching for more.

Feedback can be given and received daily, as well as more formally as part of performance or coaching conversations.

As a business owner, you also need to be open to receiving feedback from your team and to improving your own behaviour, in order to make it as easy and productive as possible for the team to work with and for you.

For teams focused on continuous improvement and business growth, receiving regular feedback from your customers is vital. You need to have a system to enable you to gather this data and to learn from it.

Feedback is a vital ingredient for business and personal growth, but only if it is listened to and acted upon positively.

Quick Questions

How easy or difficult do you find giving and receiving feedback?

Do you have a system for obtaining and acting upon feedback from your customers?

Quick Win

Here are some of the keys to the effective giving and receiving of feedback:

Giving Feedback

State the constructive purpose of your feedback. Make your purpose clear by indicating what you would like to cover and why it is important that you are initiating feedback.

'I want to discuss specifically how we communicate at our meetings – it is important that we are all in alignment and work together in the most effective way.'

Describe specifically what you have observed. Have a certain event or action in mind and be able to say when and where it happened, who was involved, and what the results were. Speak only about what you observed and avoid talking vaguely about what the person has done in the past.

'Yesterday at our meeting with our suppliers, I noticed that you raised your voice and expressed your frustrations when you gave your opinion.'

Describe your reactions. Explain the consequences of the person's behaviour and how you felt about it. Give examples of how you and others are affected.

'Our supplier sounded disappointed and surprised that she was being spoken to in this way, and I also felt uncomfortable.'

Give the other person an opportunity to respond. Remain silent and give the person a chance to explain their actions.

Or ask a question: 'What is your view of the situation?'

Listen – let them talk.

Focus on behaviour rather than the person.

Focus on what they did and how it was done, as opposed to making a comment or judgement about their personality.

This allows a person to separate their behaviour from their identity and the feedback will be less likely to be interpreted as personal criticism.

Example:

Say: 'You expressed your frustration when you gave your opinion and raising your voice can sound aggressive. I think your ideas and opinions are valid and they would come across so much better if you spoke calmly and focused on what you think works, what doesn't, and what your suggestions are.'

As opposed to:

'You are an aggressive person and I don't like it', which will probably end up as an argument.

Another example:

'You talked considerably during our recent meeting which prevented me from getting through the agenda.'

Rather than:

'You talk too much.'

Offer specific suggestions. Your feedback can include specific suggestions of a way forwards which could improve the situation. You could also ask for their suggestions.

'How do you think we could ensure that we all have airtime at our meetings and get heard properly by each other?'

Summarize and express your support. Review the main points you discussed. Summarize the action items, not the negative elements of the person's behaviour. End on a positive note.

'At least we understand each other better having talked about this. I will do what I can to make sure that I show you that your ideas and opinions have been taken on board and factored into the programme.'

Receiving Feedback

Having an open-minded attitude to receiving feedback with a willingness to learn from it is a good first step. Not everyone will have the skill and awareness to deliver feedback perfectly, so as a business owner you may need to put aside your sensitivities and realise that all feedback has a positive intention.

Someone wants things to be better and has the courage to speak up. This is an opportunity to listen and ask questions. If you can stay detached from the delivery of the feedback and hear the core message, that will help you.

Always think, 'What do I have to learn here?' and take something positive out of it. If you are not clear what the person giving you feedback means, ask questions so that you fully understand what you need to change.

Positive Feedback

When you give positive feedback, always be as specific as you can.

For example: 'You are really good at handling conflict situations – you stay calm and ask questions without any judgement at all. I can see how you detach yourself from the emotions and stay focused on the outcomes.'

Or,

'I really appreciate the speed and efficiency with which you work. I like the way you manage me so that we get the important things on the to-do list done.'

Quick Success

As a busy director of a number of growing businesses, Stuart needs to manage and give feedback on a daily basis to a number of very strong characters. Many of them find taking feedback difficult. I have seen him at work in some highly charged situations. He always stays calm and practises the winning formula. The result is he is highly respected and the teams he works with are all developing and growing successfully.

Quick Actions

Try the Quick Win suggestions next time you need to give feedback.

Give your team members some specific, positive feedback. Be open to receiving feedback yourself.

50: Track achievements and actions

'Positive reflection generates the energy to be able to take positive action.'

If you are like most business owners, you are too busy to be able to reflect on your achievements. One week merges into the next and before you know it, Christmas has come round again. If someone asked you what you had achieved during the last month, you would probably look blank and say, 'I don't know, but I worked hard.'

Reflecting on your achievements and encouraging your team to do likewise can be a very positive experience. Talking about them will automatically create a positive energy.

An achievement doesn't just have to be the point when you reach your final destination – it can be all the little things which you see en route. It may be business-related, or it may be personal, it could be a sporting interest, time with family, or time for yourself.

Focusing on achievements helps train your brain to choose activities and actions that get you where you want to be. Rather than keeping your head down, immersed in hard work, you will be able to see a light to focus on.

If you track your actions and achievements each month, you will build a powerful momentum towards your business breakthrough. See this through for a full twelve months and the goals you aspire to will become a reality.

If you combine this reflection with an attitude of gratitude for the good things that happen, you will feel even better!

Quick Questions
What have you achieved this month?

What have been your achievements this year?

Quick Win
To start to make the tracking of achievements and actions in your business work for you and your team, the formula to follow is quite simple:

Organise a monthly meeting with your team. At the start of the meeting each month, ask each person to contribute what they feel they have achieved.

Listen to each other and acknowledge the contribution each person has made.

Ask questions (as appropriate) and learn from all your team's achievements.

Include an important personal life achievement each month.

Keep a record.

At the end of the meeting, agree an action plan and allocate measurable actions for each member of the team.

Create an opportunity to report back on the achievement of these actions at the next meeting.

Make sure you balance a reflection on the positive and the milestones that have been reached before moving on to the next task.

Quick Success

I use this formula as part of my successful business mentoring process. It is why I know it works so well, as I see at first hand the energy, momentum and results it creates. I always start all my mentoring sessions with a reflection on my client's achievements for that month.

I recognise the effort that has been put in and hear their story. I emphasise the learning points by asking questions and reflecting back the essential points.

At the end of every session I encourage the setting of a clear and focused action plan. We then review the achievement of that action plan the following month. I record both my client's achievements and actions in the notes for that session.

It sounds simple, but it really does keep my clients on track for the breakthroughs they aspire too, as well as appreciating and learning from the journey.

They use this formula themselves with their teams and have enjoyed similar successful results.

Quick Actions

Every month, reflect upon and write down what you have achieved.

Write a monthly action plan which you review as part of your achievement reflection.

Appreciate and give thanks for everything you learn on your journey.

Chapter Review

Quick Wins to Build Team Talent and Support

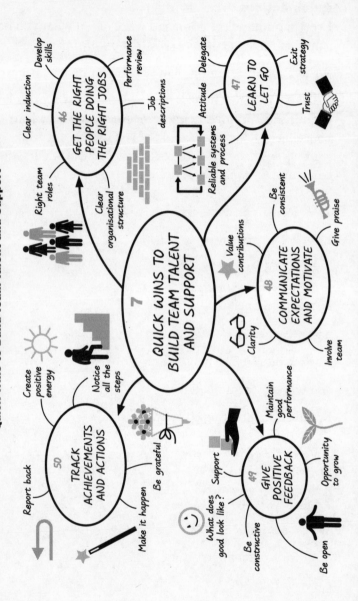

Heart of Business

If, having read this book, you wish to find out more, please email Jackie personally at jackie@heart-of-business.co.uk or jackie@jackiejarvis.co.uk. You can also read case studies and success stories at www.heart-of-business.co.uk and www.jackiejarvis.co.uk

The Heart of Business team may be able to help with:

Business mentoring

Expert training (sales, leadership, finance, management, team building, communication, presentation, time management and personal effectiveness)

Marketing strategy and practical project delivery

Market intelligence and competition research

Tele-appointment making

Brand and marketing collateral design

Print

Social media and PR

Video production

Website design

SEO and content marketing

Copywriting

CRM systems

Email marketing

Accountancy

Financial Directors

Commercial law

Exiting and selling a business

ISO 9001 consultancy

Human resources

Recruitment

Personality profiling

IT

Visit www.heart-of-business.co.uk or
www.jackiejarvis.co.uk

Good luck, and I wish you all the success you deserve.

Jackie Jarvis

Index